# FULFILLMENT OF PURPOSE

## Volume One

# Writings by Marie S. Watts

The Ultimate

Prayers and Excerpts from The Word

Success Is Normal, Just Be Yourself,
   Your Eternal Identity

Fulfillment of Purpose, Volume One

Fulfillment of Purpose, Volume Two

You Are the Splendor

Gems & Poems of The Ultimate

The Gospel According to Thomas

Three Essential Steps

The Omnipresent I Am, Volume One

The Omnipresent I Am, Evidenced, Volume Two

The Ultimate Awareness, an Eternal Constant,
   Volume One

The Ultimate Awareness, an Eternal Constant,
   Volume Two

These and other books available through:
Mystics of the World
Eliot, Maine
www.mysticsoftheworld.com

# FULFILLMENT OF PURPOSE

## Volume One

Marie S. Watts

# Fulfillment of Purpose
## Volume One
### by Marie S. Watts

Mystics of the World First Edition 2015
Published by Mystics of the World
ISBN-13: 978-0692528440
ISBN-10: 069252844X

For information contact:
Mystics of the World
Eliot, Maine
www.mysticsoftheworld.com

Photography by © Dr. Joel Murphy 2015
www.DrJMphotography.zenfolio.com
Printed by CreateSpace
Available from Mystics of the World and Amazon.com

# CONTENTS

# Introduction

Dear Reader:

These two volumes of classwork, entitled *Fulfillment of Purpose*, are being presented as the fulfillment of a definite purpose. The basis of this work is the Absolute Ultimate, and it is being written solely for those who have transcended the duality of metaphysics and have discovered that the Absolute is the only way for them. "God is All, All is God," is, of necessity, our *only* basis.

Sometimes it appears that we experience a period of uncertainty after we have left the methods—affirmations and denials—of metaphysics. No longer can we do "mental work." Yet we realize that our Consciousness must be purposefully active. We know that we cannot completely ignore the seeming problems that appear to present themselves. Neither can we accept these illusions as though they were genuine. Always these questions arise: "If I cannot do anything about these illusory problems, what should I do? What should the activity of my Consciousness be? How am I going to perceive and manifest the Perfection I know to be All?"

We are aware of the fact that we cannot *use* the Absolute. Thus, there can be no method, and sometimes it seems that we drift aimlessly and without purpose. Consequently, we often discover that our awareness of the Absolute does not seem to be evidenced in our daily affairs. In short, although we experience the sheer joy of knowing the Absolute, it may appear that we continue to be faced with problems.

There is a right way to contemplate, and this "right way" does not involve any assumptive thinking or reasoning so-called mind. Rather, it is the effortless way of simply perceiving the eternal, perfect, omniactive, omnipresent Omnipresence— God—which comprises the boundless Entirety that we call this Universe. In this right contemplation, the Absolute Truths we know are manifested in our daily affairs. Furthermore, in this right contemplation, we find that the Body does evidence the Absolute Perfection we perceive. This contemplation does not involve a method. Yet it is orderly, even as the activity of the Universe is orderly, and wonderfully simple when understood.

The purpose of this classwork is to reveal the orderly, specific way in which our contemplation fulfills its purpose. Knowledge is power. And the Mind that *knows* the way of purposeful contemplation is the Power that fulfills the purpose of this contemplation. In this way, the complete power of our "knowing" is realized, and it is evidenced in and *as* our daily affairs. Furthermore, this purposeful contemplation is manifested as the perfect Essence and Activity which comprises the Body.

In this first volume of *Fulfillment of Purpose*, we have presented the universal fact of purposeful

8

Existence. In the second volume of this classwork, this universal, purposeful, omniactive Omnipresence is specifically revealed as our daily affairs, our homes, businesses, and as all our experiences. But this perfect, joyous, free, effortless fulfillment of purpose is also revealed as the Essence and the Activity of the Body.

It is imperative to inform you, dear reader, that this first volume of classwork should be thoroughly studied and contemplated before beginning the study of the second volume. This first book is a thorough preparation for the second volume, which is very specific in its revelations. Knowing the presence of the Power of the revelations herein set forth, I now lovingly dedicate this classwork to you, the beloved, enlightened reader.

Boundless Light and Love,
Marie S. Watts

# Chapter I

# Full Open Consciousness

All of us have attended many lectures and classes. We have listened to countless words, telling us of many Truths. Yet more often than not, the words are forgotten, and we go right on seeming to experience problem after problem. Often, during a lecture or a class session, we are really inspired, and we are very sure that the Truth we seem to have been seeking is finally revealed. We are confident that now the evidence of this Truth will be forthcoming. Yet subsequent events appear to deny and defy the actuality of the Truth we have perceived so clearly. Why is it that we appear to fail to perceive—thus experience—the full and complete evidence of the Truths that have uplifted and apparently enlightened our Consciousness?

Let us now explore the answers—and there are many—to the foregoing question. We will begin this exploration with some penetrative questions. What are words? Are they necessary? Do they serve any genuine purpose? What is the origin of words? Why did they come into being? Which came first, the words or the facts that are presented in sounds and letters called words? Are words eternal or temporal? Are the Truths presented by words eternal or temporal? Can the Truth really be expressed in words? If the Truth could really be expressed in words, why is it that we would not be enlightened or inspired if we were to hear this Truth spoken in some language with which we are not familiar?

Now let us explore these questions, one by one, and see just what answers can be presented through the use of words. Words, when spoken, are a sequence of various sounds and inflections. Words, when written or printed, are a sequence of various pictures or symbols, strung together in something called sentences or paragraphs. We may listen to words spoken in a language that is foreign to us, but these words have no genuine meaning to us. They are simply sounds. In like manner, we may read words written in a language that is strange to us, and they are but meaningless pictures that portray nothing to us.

Words that present spiritual facts are symbols. They signify the Presence of the Truth But the symbol can never be the genuine expression of this Truth it symbolizes. We can perceive a simile of this fact through the consideration of music. For instance, the notes that symbolize the tones or music are merely signs that we read, signs that are symbols for the tone. But the notes are not the tones. Neither do the notes express the tones. The tones are the Truth of the Beauty called Music. Yet the notes are useful as signs that signify the Presence of the tones, the harmonies, the rhythms of Music.

In this way, we can realize that words are useful. We can perceive that they are necessary. However, we are not confused as to their purpose. We know that there is a point beyond words, and it is this silent ecstasy of wordless joy that reveals the Self to be One and One alone. This perception, of course, is illumination.

It is well to realize that words only *seem* necessary in the fallacious human sense of being. It is only because we seemed to become unaware of our glorious, complete, eternal Being that words seemed to become necessary. *The infinite, perfect, constant Truth is an Eternal Existent.* Words are only temporal expedients. They come and go, but the Truth remains forever as It is.

Actually, some of us are becoming aware of the fact that words are not necessary. We find that we can, and do, communicate without words. This has nothing to do with mental telepathy or anything pertaining to the mythical human mind. It is simply a matter of Consciousness. It is the Self-revealed fact that we are one indivisible, inseparable Consciousness. But it is also a realization of the universal, integral Nature of all Being.

The foregoing presents at least a partial explanation as to just why, so often, our attendance at classes and lectures does not seem to fulfill its purpose. But there is more to be revealed, as you will presently see.

Right now, let us perceive what should be realized in order that our lectures and classes may increasingly fulfill the purpose for which they are intended.

The most important aspect of this fulfillment is our realization of the fact that we are *One*. There really is one Consciousness, one Mind, one Life, one Love, and this inseparable All is never divided into separate consciousnesses, minds, lives, or loves. It is in our clear perception of our *inseparable oneness* that the truths revealed during any lecture or class session continue to be perceived and thus to *fulfill the purpose* for which they were revealed.

It is necessary to *know* that the speaker and the hearer are *one* inseparable, conscious, living, loving Mind. If we listen to a speaker as though he or she were a Consciousness separate from our Consciousness, we are not hearing the voice of our own Consciousness. We are not even hearing our own words.

We may agree with what we are hearing. We may even be absolutely convinced that it is true, but it will seem to be a Truth that is true as someone or something other than our own God-Self. This, of course, is duality. This brings us to the next important aspect of our lectures and classes.

It is imperative that every lecture, every class session, completely fulfill its purpose. Before any lecture or class is presented, the lecturer, or the so-called teacher, is aware of the Truths that are to be revealed. It is true that he or she may not consciously

14

realize every aspect of Truth that will be revealed during the session. Yet his or her Consciousness is actively engaged and full open for whatever Truth that should be presented. In other words, he is prepared. But it is well to realize that *we* are just as necessary to the fulfillment of the purpose of the lecture or class session as is the lecturer or speaker.

Before attending any lecture or class, we should be prepared. Yes, we should be as well-prepared as should the lecturer or the one called teacher. First of all, we should contemplate the Truth of our indivisible Oneness. We should perceive that the Consciousness of the speaker and the Consciousness that we are is the same Consciousness. We should perceive the fact that there is no barrier, no line of demarcation, between the speaker and the hearer of the Word because the Consciousness of the speaker and the Consciousness that we are is *one inseparable Consciousness.*

It will be helpful to consider the fact that every Truth that is to be revealed is already present within and *as* our own Consciousness. We are not expecting to hear some new Truth. We are not expecting to hear some Truth that is unknown to us. We do not expect to hear some Truth that is going to heal us or help us solve some problem. We are attending this lecture or this class for the sheer joy of actively perceiving the Truths we already know and *are.* Our Consciousness is "full open," and we know that whatever Truths should be revealed are already present, and *eternally present*, within and as our Consciousness. Right here—within and as our Consciousness—is where it is to be revealed.

Our presence at this event is important. Indeed, it is as important as is the presence of the lecturer or the so-called teacher. We have not chosen to attend this lecture or this class. We are to be present because we have no choice. We know whether or not to be present at any lecture or class. When we know that we should be present, we also know that we have to be present. This, of course, is our own God-Consciousness fulfilling Its purpose, and we could not resist it if we wished.

We may contemplate all of these Truths and many more, but there is at least one more Truth it would be well to consider before we arrive at any lecture or class, and this Truth is of vital importance. It is one that is rarely considered, yet a deep contemplation of this Truth—preceding any lecture or class—may very well mean the perception and the evidence of constant, conscious "seeing" and Being.

Jesus knew the tremendous significance of this Truth when he said, "I am the truth." This is the all-important Truth we should realize before we enter any hall where a lecture or class is to be given:

> I am the truth. I am not partially the Truth. I am not a limited Truth. *There is no limited Truth.* I am the complete Truth. I am the whole Truth. I am the entire Truth.

I have to be the entire Truth because the Truth is the Entirety of the *I* that I am. What Truth could possibly be revealed that I do not know and that I do not know my Self to be?

The Truth that I am is the full open Consciousness that I am, fully aware of knowing and of being every Truth that I am.

Of course, the foregoing statements are not presented as a method for contemplation. You may discover that altogether different words are appearing as the symbols for your contemplations. However, it is certainly of the utmost importance for you to go to any lecture or class session as full open Consciousness and well-prepared for any revelation to occur *within* and *as* your own Consciousness.

In like manner, it would be well to prepare your Self before reading the Bible or any spiritual literature. It is a beautiful and glorious experience to read any literature on the Absolute, when the Consciousness is full open and prepared in the foregoing way. After this kind of preparation, you will be amazed at the tremendous revelations you will experience when you attend lectures or classes and when you read statements of Absolute Truth. But this is not all, You will find that the Truths you read or hear stay right where they belong, namely, within and *as* your own Consciousness. Thus, the purpose of your reading or listening will be fulfilled. Then, too, the Truth you know your Self to be will be a constant Presence.

Now, why don't you contemplate these Truths before you read another word in this book? Try it, and see what takes place. Then continue with this contemplation just prior to opening this or any other book on the Absolute Truth. It is exceedingly helpful to realize that not only *are* you every Truth that can be revealed, but also you *know* that you are all Truth. It wouldn't help much to *be* the Truth if you did not know what you were, and are. So admit that you are the Consciousness that is *aware of being* every Truth that can be revealed, realized, and evidenced,

As you know, this book is comprised basically of the revelations we experienced during several classes entitled "Fulfillment of Purpose." Nonetheless, as always, revelations will continue to flow and surge during the writing of this book of classwork. Thus, those of you who attended the above mentioned classes will discover many Truths that were not revealed during our class sessions.

However, at this point, it would be well to consider the role of the one called "teacher" in this activity. Actually, the word *teacher* is a misnomer. This Truth cannot be taught. It can be presented in words that symbolize Its presence, but the revelation of the Absolute Truth, *beyond the words*, must be experienced within and *as* the Consciousness of the reader.

It is not surprising that when we have reached the Absolute Ultimate we have also reached the point beyond metaphysics; thus, we can no longer expect to be taught any Truth. Even in Biblical times, this point in our revelation was foreseen. In both the Old and the New Testaments, we find the statement that we must arrive at this realization. For instance: "And they shall not teach every man his neighbor, and every man his brother, saying, Know the Lord: for all shall know me, from the least to the greatest" (Heb. 8:11). We find this statement in Jeremiah and again in 1 John.

The fact that the Ultimate Absolute cannot be taught means that the one called teacher does not choose to teach this Truth. It means that he has no choice other than to be active in whatever way is revealed as his activity within and as his own Consciousness.

It is not until this irresistible impulsion is experienced that we really can present this Absolute Truth with the inspiration of absolute certainty of Its omnipresent Omnipotence. When this takes place, of course, the one who presents this Truth knows that he is not teaching it *to* anyone. He does not limit the "hearers" of the Word. Rather, he joyously acknowledges their Completeness as the very same Entirety that he knows himself to be. This is why such glorious Light reveals Itself during the class sessions and why so many so-called healings take place.

It is true that the words that symbolize the Truth do fulfill a purpose. They serve as a reminder to us. They help us to remind ourselves of the Truth we have really always known and will forever know. It is only that, for a second in the eternity of our Being, we seem to have forgotten what God is, thus, what we are. Immediately, when we hear or read these words that symbolize or represent the Truth, we know that the Truth they represent is true. We do not learn that some specific Truth is true; rather, it is as though suddenly we are reminded of a Truth we already knew.

Often we find ourselves saying, "Somehow, I have always felt that this is the way it is." What this really means is that the Consciousness we are is suddenly *actively* aware of some Truth that appears to have been dormant—for a moment in the eternity of our Being—within and as our Consciousness.

This, beloved, is why no one can choose to teach this Absolute Ultimate. We cannot say, "I have decided to teach this Truth." We have to wait until we feel such a deep, compelling impulsion to "speak the Word," that even if we wished, we could not resist; and of course, we don't wish to argue or to act in any way contrary to this glorious impulsion. However, when this irresistible, surging urge takes place, we know that the Absolute Ultimate cannot be taught to anyone. We know that the very effort to teach this Truth to anyone would defeat the entire purpose of the class activity.

Now, you may wonder why an attempt to teach this Truth would defeat the purpose of the activity. The defeat would be inevitable because the basis of the activity would be dual. It would mean the entirely fallacious situation of one Consciousness functioning as the teacher and several other Consciousnesses functioning as the students. Thus, the entire activity would be based on the false premise that Consciousness is, or can be, divided. It would imply a dividing line that separated the Consciousness of the student from the Consciousness of the teacher and vice versa. Therefore, at the very beginning of the class, there would be a false sense of limitation for the student, as well as for the so-called teacher.

But equally important is the fact that such an attitude on the part of the one called teacher would be based on the false assumption that the infinite, All-conscious. living Mind was not equally present within and as every Identity. However, when the irresistible impulsion to "speak the Word" is experienced, we can be assured that it is universal, living, conscious Mind revealing Itself *as* Itself. And we realize that we have no choice other than to speak or write as we hear. In this way, the Infinite All evidences Itself and fulfills Its purpose as Self-revelation.

Throughout the ages, we have had teachers *and* students, leaders *and* followers, masters *and* disciples. Yet it appears that we are still very far from having reached the goal of perfect, conscious *knowing* the Truth and being the evidence of the Truth we know. Furthermore, this fallacious appearance of limitation will continue until we stop limiting ourselves by falsely considering ourselves to be students, followers, or disciples. It is this apparent limitation of dualism that has seemed to act as a barrier to our own glorious Self-revelation of the Completeness which is our Entirety.

Doesn't it seem to you that *now* we should stop this fallacious, dualistic attitude and boldly, confidently, accept and claim our own Completeness? In some of the earliest writings of the Ultimate, the statement was made that "the gift of God is Himself." Let not one of us deny or refuse to accept this omnipresent gift. Let us fully and completely accept the fact that the gift of the God-Self is the complete Self of each Identity.

Above all, let us—right here and now—be very firm in our realization that the one called teacher and the one called student are one inseparable Consciousness. Thus, the one who writes and the one who reads are this same one indivisible Consciousness. In other words, I am no more conscious than you are; hence, I am no more of Consciousness than you are. In this way, you can clearly perceive the fact that God, the *only* Consciousness, is just as conscious as the Consciousness that you are, as God is conscious as the Consciousness that I am.

I have dwelt at some length on this subject of our indivisibility and of our equality because if the purpose of these classnotes is to be fulfilled, your realization of being the All-knowing, conscious Mind is necessary. And your awareness of being the all-knowing Mind is certainly necessary to this fulfillment of your purpose in reading and contemplating these Truths herein presented.

In fact, it will be exceedingly helpful for you to pause right here for a few moments and consciously realize that *you are all Truth, you are complete knowledge of all Truth, and you are completely conscious of being all Truth.* Indeed, if you were not already the Truth, you would not be reading these words, as they would have no meaning for you.

Now we are "full open." Now we are prepared for the complete Self-revelation of every Truth that is presented within the pages of this book.

# Chapter II

# Perceiving from God's Standpoint

If you are at all acquainted with the writings of the Ultimate, you know that the entire basis of this Truth is that God is All, All is God. You also realize that God is the Entirety of this Universe, and this Universe is the Entirety that is God. Thus, our first approach must always be from the standpoint of the Universe, which is God.

In our first book of classwork, entitled *Three Essential Steps*, we presented every Truth from the universal standpoint. We will not repeat that which was revealed in this first book of Classwork. But let us now pursue our exploration into the infinite subject. Let us perceive more of the importance of the universal approach. Let us realize more of why this universal approach to all Truth is of such vital importance.

When we perceive any Truth from the standpoint of the Universe, we are perceiving this Truth from God's standpoint. To perceive from God's standpoint obliterates all the phantasmal limitations that are supposed to limit and bind assumptive man. You see, the Universe is God; consequently, the Universe is infinite, boundless, immeasurable Mind, knowing what It is. This universal Mind knows no barriers, no limitations, no incompleteness.

Universal Mind is complete, entire, total, All. Being complete, this total Mind knows All that It is, and knows Itself to be All that It is. This being true, there is nothing existing in this Universe that is not God, the Universe, knowing what It is and knowing Itself to be That.

You will recall that God is reputed to have said to Moses, "I AM THAT I AM." Well, this is but another way in which God, the Universal All, reveals that It is the only I, or Identity. To paraphrase God's reputed statement to Moses, we might say, "I am that Identity" or, "That Identity is the I that I am.

Perceiving from God's standpoint, you are perceiving from the standpoint of Universal Mind—knowing what It is and knowing Itself to be All; knowing Itself to be the only Life that lives, the only Consciousness that is conscious, the only Mind that is intelligent, and the only Love that loves. In short, to perceive from God's standpoint means to be aware of completeness. It means to be aware of the limitless, boundless Nature of your entire Existence.

In our perception that we are boundless, conscious, living Mind, we are aware of being all that we are. This is our boundless, immeasurable Completeness, in which there can be no lack, nothing absent, and certainly no vacuums. It is in this same conscious Completeness that we can have no awareness of limitations. How could there be such a thing as limitation when there is no awareness of boundaries or barriers or division? There couldn't be, and there isn't any such awareness.

There is infinite Power in your contemplation when you are perceiving from God's standpoint. This limitless Power is based in your realization that you are complete, boundless, indivisible, and immeasurable. It is based in your perception that *you* are universal Mind, Intelligence, universal Activity, universal Consciousness, universal Life, and universal Love.

When you consider your Self from the standpoint of the Universe Itself, you are unlimited in every way. This means that you are aware of *being* limitless, complete health, complete joy, and peace. In this contemplation, you realize that you are complete Perfection, entirely whole and totally conscious of being immeasurably aware of all abundance.

You are aware of infinite supply as every aspect of Supply. This means limitless vigor, strength, and exuberance. It means knowing and being the very presence of anything and everything that is necessary to your completeness and to your complete fulfillment of purpose every moment. It means inexhaustible Supply in the form and substance called money. More will be revealed on this specific aspect of Supply in another section of this book. For the present, it is sufficient to state that money is not the kind of substance it appears to be.

In any event, you can now realize that contemplation from the universal standpoint means that you are inexhaustible and that you cannot be depleted. You cannot be measured, divided, or bound. There simply are no limitations at all when you see from this boundless, immeasurable standpoint.

Now, let us assume for a moment that we were to approach this Truth from the so-called personal little "I" standpoint. Of course, we know that this is totally illusory because there really is no "person." There really is but one *I*, and this certainly is not a little personal identity. However, for the purpose of clarification, we will briefly explore the futility of attempting to contemplate any Truth from this false standpoint.

We know that there are some sincere students who feel that meditation is the right way for them. They will literally "pull in" their attention and try to concentrate at one small point. Then they will attempt to extend or expand their Consciousness outward from this tiny point. We have no criticism of this approach or for those who practice it. But this is not the way of the Ultimate.

We cannot begin our contemplation by concentrating the attention of the so-called human mind at one small pinpoint. Rather, we are at once "full open" Consciousness, and we do not concentrate or limit our Consciousness in any way. We know that if we were to start with limitation, our perception would naturally be limited. In order that the boundless, complete, universal Mind may reveal Its limitless Self to be our Self, we realize the necessity to keep our Consciousness completely free from any limitation.

We are aware of the fact that if we were to draw an imaginary, tiny circle around our Self at the very beginning of our contemplation, all we could hope for or expect to experience would be a slightly larger circle. Still we would be limited and bound by the circle. Starting with limitation, we will surely be limited in what we perceive; thus, we will also be limited in the evidence of the Truth we perceive.

We must maintain a limitless, boundless premise in our contemplation if we are to perceive our boundless Being and if we are to experience the evidence of complete freedom from illusory bondage in every aspect of our entire Existence.

# Chapter III

# Life: A Universal Constant

When we perceive Life from the universal standpoint, we can clearly see that Life cannot begin, nor can It end. We are aware that we are completely free from all so-called illusions of a human life that is limited to what the world calls some seventy years —the threescore and ten years supposedly allotted to man.

What a tragic fallacy this illusion is for those of us who do not yet seem to be aware of our eternal, boundless, immeasurable Life. However, when we perceive Life from Its limitless standpoint, all we can see, all we can know is the complete, eternal, infinite, universal Life. And we know that this Life is the *only* Life that is ever alive.

Perceiving eternal Life from this infinite standpoint, we are aware of the fact that Life is omnipresent. Actually, Life is a universal, constant Omnipresence. Realizing this fact, it is impossible to imagine a vacuum in which there is no Life.

Today, even the physicists recognize the fact that Life exists on planets that were heretofore considered incapable of sustaining Life. One of our leading physicists has stated that there are literally millions of planets in our Milky Way that are capable of sustaining Life, very much the same as it is sustained on our Earth Planet. The nuclear physicists have made discoveries of even greater importance to the realization that Life is a Universal Constant. They now know that the atmosphere—even in what they call "outer" space—is literally teeming with activity, and this activity is apparent as substance in forms. What they are inferring is that structural Life, or Life in form, exists throughout the entire so-called space area they have explored. We realize that these deductions are based entirely from an illusory, material standpoint. Nonetheless, they are symbolic of the spiritual fact that Life is a Universal Constant.

Of course, it is not our intention to explore—or attempt to explain—the discoveries of the physicists. However, we cannot completely ignore or discount these discoveries because gradually they, too, are arriving at the inevitable conclusion that matter—as it appears to be—is an illusion.

They have also discovered the nucleus at the center of the atom. They know that it consists of Light. It is true that they have not as yet interpreted this Light to be Life. Yet Light is Life, and one day these dedicated individuals will realize that they have discovered Life Itself.

Their discovery of the fact that matter is an illusion means that they are arriving at an entirely new concept of Substance. And ultimately the physicists—as well as all of us—must inevitably realize that all Substance is Spirit, Consciousness. In addition to this, the Light — nucleus — which they know to be at the center of the atom, must finally be recognized to be Life Itself. Light *is* Life, even as Life is Light.

Some of the nuclear physicists maintain that the air is filled with atomic structures. Well, a structure would have to have form. This Light which *is* Life does exist in and as Form. But Life also exists in and as Substance. Thus, Life exists as Substance in Form, universally and eternally.

Right here, we must be very alert that we do not permit any false sense of division or separation to deceive us. Although it is true that living Substance does exist within and as Its specific Form, Life is indivisible. But it is well to realize that the actual Substance Itself is also indivisible. Elsewhere in the writings of the Ultimate, you will discover how it is, and why it is, that living Substance can be — and is — manifested within and *as* a specific Form, and yet this living Substance is indivisibly omnipresent.

For the present purpose, suffice it to say that the universal All does not divide Itself, despite the fact that It is only an illusory appearance of living Substance in Form that manifests Itself in — and as — specific Forms, and that seems to present a false picture of that which is inseparable. It all has to do with the infinite variety in which God — the All — identifies and evidences Itself.

Life, in order to be Life, has to be alive. It has to live. If Life did not live — if It were not alive — there would be no purpose in Its being. Life does live. But in order that Life be alive, it has to be alive as Something, some Essence. It is alive as Something, and this Something is Its own Substance, which is Spirit—Consciousness. There would be no Life — and no purpose fulfilled as Light—if Life were not alive as Substance. *There could be no Life if there were no Substance to be alive.* This Substance which is alive exists in and as Form everywhere and eternally. This being true, it follows that Universal Life is an omnipresent, eternal, Universal Constant.

Einstein has said, "Light is a universal constant." Well, as stated before, Light is Life. And since Light is a Universal Constant, it follows that Life is a Universal Constant. This is true because Light and Life are one and the same Essence and Activity. As Life—Light—is a Universal Constant, the structure—Form—that is essential to the fulfillment of Life's purpose must, of necessity, be constantly present.

But Life—Light—is also an *eternal* Constant. This being true, the Essence in Form that is alive, that lives, is as eternal as is Life Itself. How, then, could there be a temporary body? There is no body that begins and ends. There is no Substance, no Life, no Mind that begins and ends. Therefore, that which has appeared to be a born body is not valid. It is neither Substance, Life, nor Form. It follows then, that a body that seems to become ill, old, deteriorate and disintegrate, is completely false. It is illusion, and we have seemed to be deceived by this illusion quite long enough.

Now, we have discussed Universal Life. We have perceived that It is not limited in so-called time or space. We have realized that Life does not divide Itself through Its identification of Itself, nor does It separate Itself through Its formation of Itself as an infinite variety of forms, designs, or patterns. It makes no difference what the Form, or evidence, of Life may be—it has to be indivisible Life in Form.

Life, Consciousness, Mind, Love, bespeak the Whole that is God. When we contemplate these four words, we realize that all that God is, is symbolized by these four little words. This, of course, is the Entirety of your Being and of your Body. God really is All; All really is God. And there is nothing other than God for you to know or to be. Indeed, living, conscious, intelligent Love is alive this moment *as* the eternal Substance that you are.

# Chapter IV

# Perception: A Universal Constant

Let us now contemplate the inseparable aspect of Life that is Consciousness. Soul, Spirit, Consciousness, are exactly the same Essence. In this same way, Consciousness and Life are inseparably One. There can be no Life without Consciousness.

Neither can there be Consciousness without Life. And right here it should be clear that the same Truth is true as Mind—or Intelligence—and as Love. Conscious, living, loving Mind is one constant, inseparable Essence, and there is no way in which this indivisible Essence can be separated into essences. From the foregoing, you can see that every Truth that is true as Life is also true as Consciousness, as Mind, and as Love.

Sometimes there seems to be some confusion about this word *Consciousness*. To many, it has a human or mortal connotation; but Consciousness is universal, conscious, living Mind, and this Infinity could never be the *assumed* consciousness of an illusory mortal or human. The very nature of an illusory human mind or consciousness is limited. But Consciousness is completely unaware of limitation of any kind or nature.

You see, virtually all our seeming difficulty stems from the illusion that we became conscious human beings, each one of us with a separate human consciousness. This leads to the further mistake that we are conscious as human or temporary mortal beings, functioning under all the false laws and limitations of this illusion. However, this entire illusion — with all of its limitations and cruelties — disperses when, in illumination, we are aware of being universally conscious as well as of being Universal Consciousness Itself.

The foregoing brings us to a very important aspect of all our "seeing." So often, someone will say, "Oh, I know the Truth about this situation or about myself, but somehow the evidence of what I know is not apparent." The words may vary, but the meaning remains the same. So long as we still seem to be a human consciousness knowing the Truth, it is going to continue to appear that we are knowing the Truth *about* some so-called condition or *about* an Identity.

When, in contemplation, we are knowing any specific Truth, there should be — and is — a definite purpose in our contemplative knowing. This glorious purpose can never be fulfilled completely, or evidenced, so long as we seem to be merely knowing the Truth *about* anything or anyone. It is always the little, limited, illusory human mind or consciousness that imagines it can know the Truth about anything or anyone. But this limited, assumptive, little mind can really know nothing of Truth. It is not conscious because it is not Consciousness.

Consciousness does not know the Truth *about* anything or anyone. Consciousness is aware of *being* the Truth. Furthermore, Consciousness is aware of the unalterable fact that everything and everyone *is* the Truth. Thus, Consciousness is aware of being the Truth that constitutes the Entirety of every One and every Thing. Being consciously Universal Perfection, It—Consciousness—can have no awareness of "conditions." It is completely unconditioned, constant, perfect Being. This Universal Consciousness is aware of *being* All that It sees, perceives, or knows.

Perfect awareness of Being is very different from knowing the Truth about something or someone. Universal Awareness of Being is the indivisible, infinite Consciousness aware of distinction manifested as Its variety of Itself. *But this infinite Consciousness has no awareness of separateness or division.*

There is distinction, but there is no division. It has no awareness of any more or any less Truth. It is conscious of being equally that which is true — constantly, infinitely, and eternally. This, beloved, is Consciousness. This is the Consciousness you really have and *are*.

When we contemplate Truth conscious of *being* the Truth we know, our contemplation may very well be somewhat like that which follows:

I know the Truth. The Truth I know, I am. I am conscious of being every Truth I know. The consciousness I am—knowing and being the Truth—is the very Substance of Everyone and Everything.

The Substance of Everything and Everyone is the Consciousness that I am—knowing and being the Truth that I know. The Consciousness that is "this" Identity, this *I* that I am, already knows every Truth that I know and am.

This is true because the Consciousness of this Identity and the Consciousness that I am are one inseparable Universal Consciousness.

Of course, the foregoing is not to be used as a method or formula for so-called treatment. There are innumerable revelations that will surge and flow as your Consciousness when you contemplate from this universal standpoint. What has just been presented is only for the purpose of bringing to your attention the importance of the realization of being the indivisible Universal Consciousness in all your contemplation.

Needless to say, there is no false sense of "doing" anything about some seeming inharmony in this contemplation. Rather, it is simply a calm, firm, unshakable conviction of the *one* and *only* Presence and Power. But above all, there is an awareness of *being* this universal, omnipotent Presence. And there is also a tremendous awareness that Everyone and Everything is this same indivisible Presence and Power.

*Consciousness is Substance.* The Consciousness you are, contemplating the Truth you know, is the only Substance present *as* your Body. Oh! If you perceive the wonderful, limitless scope of this kind of contemplation, you may rest assured that the purpose of your contemplation will be completely fulfilled, and the evidence of the Perfection you are seeing will be manifest as your Being.

From the foregoing, you can perceive the importance of the word *Consciousness.* Hence, you can realize the vital necessity to realize that you are the Truth, the Substance, the Life, Mind, Love, *as* the manifestation of all that you are knowing.

There is one more aspect of Consciousness that we must explore. We have stated that it is necessary to realize that you are the Truth you are knowing and contemplating. We have also stated that Consciousness is the only Substance in existence. Thus, Consciousness is the Substance of the *only* Body in existence.

The Truth is that which is true. To know the Truth means to know that which is true.

> The Consciousness you are, aware of the Truth, is the Substance you are, aware of being the Truth.

Consciousness, aware of being the Truth, is conscious awareness of only that which is true. Consciousness, aware of being the Truth, is Conscious awareness of being *only* that which is true and of nothing else. Truth is eternal, constant, Absolute Perfection. Therefore, that which is true is eternal, constant, Absolute Perfection.

It is our Consciousness that enables us to know that we exist. If we were not conscious, we would have no awareness of Being. But because we are conscious, we know that we exist. We even know that we exist as an Identity. There is nothing that can be conscious but Consciousness, and Consciousness fulfills Its purpose by being conscious, eternal, perfect, constant. Consciousness fulfills Its purpose by being eternally, constantly perfect as the Consciousness you are and that I am.

Consciousness has no choice when it comes to being the Truth It knows. This is absolutely true. You see, Consciousness is the Substance of the Truth It is knowing. Thus, it has to *be* that which is true, the true and only Substance. Consciousness, which is the only Substance of the Body, does know that which is true—the Truth—and thus, Consciousness, the only Substance of the Body, has to be the true Substance.

You have often stated that you are the Truth. Now it is necessary to realize that the Body Itself is the Truth. The Consciousness, Substance, that is the Body is aware of being only the Truth—or of being that which is true. Thus, the Substance of the Body is constantly, eternally aware of *being* eternal, constant Perfection. Conscious, eternal, constant, Absolute Perfection is the true and only Substance. The Body, consisting of Consciousness, is aware of being the true and only Substance, which is conscious, eternal, constant, Absolute Perfection.

Beloved, I cannot tell you in words how important the entire section of this book dealing with Consciousness will prove to be in your knowing the Truth and in consciously *being* the Truth you know. Consequently, I lovingly recommend quite an intensive and earnest study and contemplation of this particular section of these classnotes.

# Chapter V

# Mind: A Universal Constant

Now we have arrived at the word *Mind,* which symbolizes Universal Intelligence. We have discussed Life and Consciousness. We have perceived their inseparable nature. We have realized that Life is alive as Consciousness—Substance—and that living Consciousness is the living Substance of Everyone and Everything. We know that living Consciousness is an eternal Universal Constant. Now let us perceive that Mind—Intelligence—is also an eternal Universal Constant. In this way, we can easily realize the inseparability of Life, Consciousness, and Mind.

This is a purpose-full Universe. Universal Life fulfills Its purpose by being eternally, constantly alive. Universal Consciousness fulfills Its purpose by being eternally, constantly conscious. Universal Mind—Intelligence—fulfills Its purpose by being eternally, constantly intelligent. We know that Consciousness is a living, active, Universal Substance, or Essence. We are also aware of the fact that this Universal Activity is an intelligent Activity. It has to be Intelligence in action because it is an *eternal, constant Existent.*

If Activity as this Universe were not intelligent, the entire Universe would have been destroyed eons ago through its own chaotic, unintelligent activity. In fact, we could draw an analogy from the seemingly unintelligent way in which the assumptive peoples of our world of today are appearing to act. Of course, we know that this is entirely illusory, but we must also realize that any activity that appears to be unintelligent—or destructive—is also illusion.

However, there is but one Truth that is true as Universal Intelligence. Being entirely intelligent, It constantly acts intelligently. It is in this way that Mind fulfills Its purpose in being and fulfills it perfectly and intelligently.

As an example of this Truth, let us turn to our friends, the leading physicists and astronomers. Although they disagree on many points pertaining to this Universe, they are all agreed on one point, and this agreement is that this is a purposeful Universe. Actually, this would not be an intelligent Universe if there were no purpose in Its being.

Again and again we have said, "God is Mind." And there could be no greater Truth. Now we are to begin to realize the tremendous universal Nature of God, the Universal Mind or Intelligence. We are to perceive that an unintelligent Universe is as impossible as would be an unintelligent God because God *is* this Universe.

Few of us seem to realize the tremendous importance of intelligent Omniaction, or omnipresent Mind in action as an eternal Universal Constant. Really, during every period of contemplation, the perception of this aspect of Truth should be considered within and as our Consciousness. This is true because activity is always present, whether it be bodily activity or the activity of our daily affairs. Wherever there seems to be any difficulty, it is well to consider the eternal fact that *Universal Mind, intelligently active, is the only activity that is present or that is going on.* This Absolute Truth is as omnipresent as is the activity of the Body, because Absolute Truth is present as the activity in the home, the business, the profession, or in any aspect of our daily living.

When we are contemplating specifically any Truth that is true as the Body, it is, however, essential to realize the indivisibility of Mind, Life, Consciousness. This is true because the Substance of the Body consists of living, intelligent Consciousness, and Its activity *is* this living, conscious Mind in constant intelligent action. Perfect Intelligence has to act perfectly. Perfection can only act as what It is. It cannot act as what It is not. It fulfills Its purpose by being intelligently, universally active—constantly, eternally, here, and now.

The following statement is of vital importance to all of our perception:

Mind knows the Truth—that which is true—
that It is. But Consciousness is Awareness.
Consciousness is aware of being the Truth—that
which is true—here, now, constantly, and eternally.

> Consciousness and Mind are inseparably One, so the knowing and the being are One. The Being of that which is true is simultaneous with the knowing of that which is true. It is always perfect, conscious, living Mind, knowing what It is and being that which It knows.

It is always essential to contemplate with the realization that we are conscious, living, perfect Mind, constantly, eternally, knowing what we are and consciously being what we know. This is Mind in action. This is conscious Existence in action. This is Life in action. This is living, conscious Intelligence eternally, constantly fulfilling Its purpose as our activity, right here and now.

Considering any Truth—anything that is true—from the Universal standpoint always dissolves all seeming barriers or limitations. In this way, we can see that the Universal Mind we are is complete, entire, All-knowing, complete knowledge. This is a complete Universe. In fact, Completeness is a Universal Eternal Constant. God—this complete Universe—must, of necessity, fulfill Its purpose by being complete as every aspect of Itself. Completeness is a universal fact, and this universal fact has to be fulfilled as our Entirety, or Completeness.

This means complete knowledge, complete joy, peace, harmony, perfection, and complete awareness of *being* all Truth, or all that is true. All knowledge is true knowledge, and there is no knowledge that is not the knowledge of that which is true.

All true knowledge is ever-present within and as the conscious, living Mind that we are. This being true, it follows that never can we be in doubt as to what to say, how to say it, or where and when to say it. Neither can we wonder what course of action we should pursue. Never do we have to "make up our mind" about anything. We know, and we know that we know. Being the Mind that is all-knowing—all knowledge—we can and do know anything that is necessary for us to know at any given moment.

I am very sure that we all have seen the proof of this fact in one way or another. It has happened that suddenly, when confronted with some unexpected situation, we knew what to say or what to do. If, one moment before, we had been asked what we would say or do in such a situation, we would probably have said that we couldn't imagine what our response would be.

Oh, we see proofs of this omnipresent Mind that we are almost every day. Complete Mind, completely intelligent, is the Mind that we constantly are. There is no other mind and no incomplete intelligence for us to have or to be.

All of this, of course, means that we are the boundless, limitless Intelligence that always knows what It should know, that knows how to act, when to act, and that always acts perfectly and intelligently. In this way, it is utterly impossible for us to make any mistake.

Right now it would be well to remind our Self of some few salient facts pertaining to contemplation. It is well to begin all contemplation from the Universal—or God—standpoint. Furthermore, it is helpful to consider the glorious fact that:

> We are the Universal Mind knowing what It is, and we are the Universal Consciousness aware of being what It knows.

Thus, we can never be engaged in absolute contemplation from a little, false, personal standpoint. It is not until we are aware that we do not even exist as a separate little person that we can realize the boundless, universal, conscious Mind that we are. Needless to say, we cannot contemplate from the Universal standpoint for any little selfish purpose. We cannot even contemplate from this standpoint so long as there seems to be some personal objective to be gained or attained. It is only the *unselfed* Universal Self that can know what It is and that can be aware of being the Truth It knows Itself to be.

As this section of the book is studied and contemplated, ever greater and more glorious revelations will be experienced. Just let the full open, conscious, living Mind surge and flow within and as the infinite *I* that is ever present, and there will be joy beyond words.

Above all, be aware of the fact that:

> You and I and all are every truth that has been revealed, that is being revealed, or that will

ever be revealed, and we are aware of *being* all that is true.

In this realization, the purpose of this book will be fulfilled. Furthermore, the purpose in reading this book will be beautifully and completely fulfilled.

Here it is, beloved. *It is you; it is me; yes, it is all there is of us—here, now, and eternally.*

# Chapter VI

## Love: A Universal Constant

We have now discussed limitless Universal Consciousness, Life, Mind. We have perceived that Life fulfills Its purpose by being eternally, constantly alive. We realize that Universal Consciousness fulfills Itself by being eternally, constantly conscious. In this same way, we know that Universal Mind fulfills Its purpose by being eternally, constantly intelligent. Thus, we are aware of the fact that living, conscious Intelligence fulfills Its purpose by being eternally, constantly, intelligently, consciously alive.

There is one more aspect of the Infinite All and Its fulfillment of purpose that we must now explore. Even though we may clearly perceive the Entirety of living, conscious Mind, our perception would indeed be incomplete if we were not aware of Love. In fact, without Love, all our "seeing" would be futile.

You see, Love is the Power. Love is the inseparable Oneness of every aspect of the Universal All. Without Love, dualism would be rampant, and we would be only innumerable little persons and things, warring with each other. Furthermore, without Love, each little personal self would be interested only in its own separate, personal aggrandizement, wealth, power, and all that makes illusory "man with breath in his nostrils" so obnoxious.

Indeed, without Love, this glorious Universe would be in complete chaos. If Love were not a Universal Constant, even the stars and planets would be warring against each other. It is Love fulfilling Its purpose that maintains this marvelous Universe in complete harmony. Above all, it is Love actively fulfilling Its purpose that intelligently acts as the perfect, harmonious Omniaction which governs Itself as this Universe.

We have perceived the necessity to be consciously aware of *being* Life, Consciousness, Mind. It goes without saying that it is also necessary to realize that we *are* Love. In fact, it is utterly impossible to know the genuine Nature of Love until, or unless, we know that *we are Love Itself*. Once we know that we are Love, we have to love, we have to be loving. We have no choice other than to *be* the Love we are.

Oh, there is tremendous power in the realization and experience of being Love Itself. But never will we be aware of being this glorious Presence if we seem to cling to a little, selfish, divisional illusion of human love. An entire book could be written on the complete fallacy of human love.

It is pointless to dwell upon that which is not. We seem to know too much about the illusion, anyway. So let us obliterate it from all consideration and perceive that universal, eternal, constant Presence which does exist.

It is in this revelation that we realize we do not give Love. Neither do we receive Love. Rather, we *are* Love, and we can no more help being Love than we can avoid being Life, Mind, Consciousness. In this same way, we are conscious of being Love.

There is a vast difference in *being* Love and in seeming to be *in* love. To personalize Love would mean to divide this omnipresent, omnipotent, constant Presence. Love is forever indivisible, immutable, beginningless, and endless. Love is eternally and constantly equal, omnipotently and omnipresently. Love can never be separated into "loves." It can never be any more or any less present. It simply *is*, and *we are it.*

Love is Perfection. Without Love there would be no Perfection. It is not just happenstance that the expression "perfect love" is frequently found in our Bible. Love, in order to be Love, has to be perfect. This is true because the only Love in Existence is perfect Love. But it is well to realize that perfect Love also means Absolute Universal Perfection. This means that perfect Love is manifested as perfect Life, perfect Health, perfect Peace and Joy—perfect Existence in every way. It means that perfect Love is the presence of perfect Activity, and above all, this Perfection which is Universal Love is the fulfillment of Its purpose in being.

Our Bible states that "perfect love casteth out fear," and that he that fears "is not made perfect in love." When we know, really know, that we are perfect Love, there cannot possibly be any awareness of fear. In this glorious perception, we are conscious of nothing that can possibly arouse fear. There is nothing existing outside of, or other than, our own God-Consciousness being Love. And Love, by Its very Nature, cannot possibly be harmful.

In this way, we perceive and experience the evidence of perfect Love in action. We see this wonderful Presence actively fulfilling Its purpose in our home, our business, our profession, our social activities, and in every aspect of our daily affairs.

Yes, we can go farther than this: we also see the evidence of perfect Love in, through, and as the Body. Make no mistake about this — perfect Love does fulfill Its purpose as the perfect, harmonious activity which is forever present within and as the Body of every one of us. However, to be fully aware of the evidence of this Love, we must perceive that It is universal and it is indivisible. It cannot seem to be love for a person or a thing to the exclusion of anyone or anything. We recognize that there are *no other* identities outside of, or other than, the conscious Love we are.

Love, in order to be perfect Love, must be Love without an object. The very moment we attempt to personalize Love, we have seemed to encircle It. We imagine that we have drawn a limiting circumference around it. In this way, we appear to have limited it; thus, it could not be the completeness of inseparable, perfect Love. If we seem to limit Love by personalizing It, we are also going to limit the power of Love.

Of course, we know that it is impossible for us to do anything to, or about, Love. It is only in the illusory seeming that we can even appear to encircle or to limit Love. The point at issue is that omnipotent Love is realized, experienced, and evidenced when we are aware of being universal, boundless, perfect, indivisible Love Itself.

Does the foregoing mean that we are not to love our families or friends? Indeed no! Nothing could be further from the Truth. We love—oh, how we love! But we do not divide the Love that we know our God-Self to be.

Love is a universal, omniactive, purpose-full Presence. This perfect, universal, constant Love fulfills Its purpose by being *active*. If we did not love our family and friends, everyone and everything, this perfect Love would not be actively fulfilling Its purpose. But this is not all. If we did not love everyone and everything equally, Love would be active only insofar as our immediate family, friends, and the like were concerned. This would be partial Love, and because Love is impartial, it would not be Love at all. Nonetheless, perfect Love does fulfill Its purpose by acting, by being loving, compassionate, and understanding.

Love is never harsh. Rather, It is ever gentle. While Love is compassionate, It never comes down to the level of the seeming problem to sympathize with the illusion, or the problem. Rather, Love understands how real the illusion can *seem* to be and simultaneously perceives that actually there is no problem and no one who is aware of having a problem. This is *intelligent*, loving compassion, and there is tremendous power in this activity of omnipotent, perfect Love.

Actually, loving in this wonderful way can be compared to watching one who is asleep and having a nightmare. We are aware of what the nightmare is presenting. We know that the nightmare may seem to be fear, pain, danger, or even a threat to Life. Yet even though we are aware of the nature of the illusory nightmare, we are also aware of the perfectly safe individual resting calmly on the bed.

We perceive that the Identity is not in the nightmare. Neither is the nightmare going on within or as his experience. It is clear that throughout the entire illusion, this one remains completely free of every picture that is presented by the fallacious nightmare. Even so, we do not harshly or rudely awaken the sleeper. Rather, we understand that the dream or illusion does seem to be very real indeed at the moment, and we are gentle and compassionate.

Needless to say, we do not try to do anything about the false pictures of the nightmare. We don't sympathize with the imaginary figure that appears to be the person in the nightmare. Rather, our entire consideration is with the one who must rise from his seeming dream, completely free and joyous.

Throughout the entire illusion, he has remained wholly intact, untouched by any of the illusory pictures of the nightmare. We are always aware of this fact. We know that we cannot even help him to get out of a situation that he never was in or knew anything about.

For instance, he was never in danger of falling off a cliff or of being pursued by something destructive. He never needed to be saved or rescued from some apparent danger that never actually was included in his experience.

Oh, there is much more that will be revealed within and as your own Consciousness, as you study and contemplate the foregoing simile. But of the greatest importance is the fact that you will be more and more aware of being Love Itself. And you will really *love*.

Someone has said, "Teach me to love." Truly, we cannot be taught to love. Love cannot be taught; neither can It be learned. Love can only be experienced, and this is the experience of *being* Love. No one can compel himself to love. No one can avoid being Love. Love simply *is*. It is you, and you are It.

Oh, if we will only perceive and experience the awareness of being Universal Love, the full evidence of this Consciousness is inevitable. To experience being the universality of Love, in all Its greatness, means to experience being the power of this selfless, impersonal Love. It is in the *conscious experience* of *being* universal, omnipotent Love that we perceive and experience the *evidence* of being Love Itself. It is evidenced as perfect harmony in every aspect of our daily affairs. Love is harmony. All of us are aware of the perfect harmony that reigns supreme with those who love unselfishly and impersonally. It is only when impersonal Love is misinterpreted and appears to be personal love that inharmony can appear in the experience of those who really love.

Harmony is heaven, and heaven is exactly what we experience when we know that we *are* Universal Love. It is Love that maintains each star and each planet in complete harmony. There is no strife in heaven. Each star and planet fulfills its purpose lovingly and harmoniously in perfect order, peace, and harmony. There is no friction between the stars and planets.

Do you know that this is a Universe of Music? Do you know that there is no vacuum anywhere that is devoid of Music? This is Absolute Truth. There is not so much as a pinpoint in this glorious, harmonious Universe that is not literally surging and flowing as perfect, indescribably beautiful Music.

Innumerable Identities have heard the "music of the spheres." It is not only students of Truth who have heard — and do hear — this Universal Music. Some of us hear It constantly. With some, it is just an occasional experience. Yet the Music is a Universal Constant, present everywhere and eternally. Furthermore, this glorious Music is equally present everywhere and eternally.

Actually, it can be said without equivocation that this Universe is one beautiful, constant, eternal Symphony. It surges and flows as complete harmony. It is rhythmic. Never does It cease to be completely harmonious. Neither is Its rhythmic activity interrupted or obstructed. Every tone that exists within and as this Universal Symphony remains that specific tone and no other. Yet every tone is comprised of the entirety of the Universal Music. Each tone is absolutely essential to the completeness that is the omnipresent Symphony. Yet the Universal Symphony is absolutely essential to the very existence of every tone.

Let us for a moment consider this symphonic Entirety as we consider the Color which is omnipresent within and as this Universe. Many of us have seen — and do see — the Allness which is the Symphony of Color. We are aware of the fact that there is distinction of color. Each color is that specific color and no other. Yet all the colors that comprise the complete, universal color Symphony are present within and *as* each specific color.

When we see this Universe as that aspect of Itself which is color, we perceive that there are no lines of demarcation between colors. These colors are not separated by any harsh lines or boundaries. Rather, it appears that a Universal Oneness makes one glorious blend of glorious, inseparable Color. It is not so much that the colors blend as it is that they are inseparably One. No matter how innumerable the colors may be, and are, the Color is all One, and there is never any inharmony between the colors because they are not separated. There could be nothing between them; they are all One, *although visible as an infinite variety of specific colors.*

In the universal symphonic Harmony—Oneness —of Color, we see that there is distinction, but there is no separation. Likewise, in the Universal Symphony of Music, we hear that there is distinction of tone, rhythm, harmonies; yet there is no division. Color is one universal, inseparable Entirety, although appearing as an infinite variety of Itself. Music is one universal, inseparable Entirety—Symphony— although this Music appears as an infinite variety of Itself.

To those of us who have studied and performed music as dedicated musicians, a Bach fugue is the most perfect symbol, or example, of this Universal Oneness of Music. This accounts for the fact that the music of Bach is generally considered to be the most perfect music that has ever been composed. Indeed, it is the closest approach to Perfection because it is the most spiritual.

Musicians the world over, some of whom are not even students of Truth, have repeatedly said that the compositions of Bach are more spiritual than is any other music. Of course, we are not attempting to confuse so-called human music with the Music of the Spheres. But it is well to consider that Bach had to hear this Music before he could write it, play it, or have it performed.

This same fact is true of every great composer and of the Music he first heard, played, and wrote. The distinction rests in the fact that the Music of Bach, as he heard it and subsequently wrote it, was —and is—more evident as Perfection and Harmony. It is Perfection and Harmony that comprise the Music of the Spheres.

Now, let us perceive just exactly why we have spoken at such great length on the subjects of Music and Color. You will remember that our subject just now is Love. We have said that Love is Perfection. We have realized that Love is Harmony. Above all, we have perceived that Love is our inseparable Oneness.

We know that Love is an omniactive Universal Constant, eternal and changeless. Thus, it is clear that Love is ever active. All that we have said of Love is true of Music. All that we have said of Music is true as Color. All that is true as the glorious Universal Symphony is true as *your* Universe. All that is true of each tone in the Universal Symphony is true as each Identity.

There is distinction within and *as* the Universal Identity, but there is no separation. And it is in this Absolute Truth that we perceive the perfect Universal Harmony, Perfection, Love in action that is your Identity. It is not that you are one *with* each Identity. Oh, no! It goes much further than such duality.

Rather, it is that every Identity is the same perfect, harmonious, eternal Consciousness that you are, and you are the very same Universal Consciousness that exists *as* every Identity. Yet with Identity, even as with Music, there is *one Identity, even as there is one Music.* Color is One. Music is one indivisible One. Identity is one inseparable One—and there is no other.

In our former book of classwork, *Three Essential Steps*, you will find the statement, "Your Consciousness is your Universe. Your Universe is your Consciousness." No greater statement of Truth could be presented than the foregoing.

It is true that you, as a distinct Identity, do exist. Yet it is also true that *there is but one universal, inseparable Identity, and you are It*. All the glorious, perfect Truth that comprises this Universe exists as your Identity. But *you* are just as necessary to the Completeness that is this Universe as is the Entirety that is this Universe necessary to your Completeness. Even as in every distinct color each color exists, so it is that all Identity exists within and *as* the distinct Identity that you are.

Every Truth is a Universal Truth. This means that every Truth is equally present everywhere and constantly as this Universe. The Truth we have just revealed as Color, as Music, as Identity, is a Universal Truth, and It is equally present infinitely and eternally. This being true, this Truth is true as you, as your Consciousness, as your Universe.

Now it is clear why there is no inharmony in the heavens. You can see why it is impossible that there should be inharmony existing within and as this Universe of innumerable stars, planets, etc. Oh, I know it is mistakenly believed that planets and stars do collide, separate, erupt, explode, etc. But this is only an extension of the so-called imperfect vision and human reasoning of "man with breath in his nostrils." And there is no such man. Thus, we will not discuss this erroneous fabrication. Nonetheless, you will marvel at the way infinite Universal Love will be evident within and as your experience when you are aware of being the perfect, harmonious Entirety which is Universal Love.

We have stated that the awareness of being Love would be evidenced in your entire experience. Indeed, this is true. You will find this Truth evidenced as a perfect, harmonious home, as a perfectly harmonious business or profession. You will perceive the evidence of this Truth in action, not only as your home and your business or professional affairs, but also in your social affairs. And above all, your Body will be the perfect evidence of the fact that you know your Self to be universal, perfect Love. Oh, you will be amazed. It is all so very beautiful, so perfect, and so completely harmonious.

Now, you may wonder just what the realization that you are Universal Love has to do with your Body. Beloved, *it has everything to do with your Body*. You see, your Body consists of the Consciousness you are; and whatever you are conscious of being, this Body is also conscious of being. You, aware of being the Universal Love that is ever perfect and harmonious, are the very Essence of your Body, knowing that It is universal, perfect Love, forever harmonious and gloriously beautiful.

Now we have arrived at the zenith of all that has gone before in this book. We have explored Universal Life, Mind, Consciousness, Love. We have perceived their Oneness. We have realized that *we are* this universal Life, Mind, Consciousness, Love. Now we can perceive and state unequivocally:

> I am universal, conscious, intelligent Love and nothing else.

Furthermore, we will know that this is the Truth that we *are*; and above all, we will know *why* this is all that is true as the Identity we are. Now we realize that we exist as the fulfillment of a Universal Purpose. We also know that we exist as the fulfillment of a specific, or distinct, Purpose. We do not attempt to separate ourselves from the universal fulfillment of Purpose any more than the drop of water in the wave tries to separate itself from the wave of the ocean and its fulfillment. In other words, we move within and *as* the Universal All rather than as a little, separate mortal trying to be something or to do something of or by a helpless little self.

As you know, the subject or title of this book is *Fulfillment of Purpose*. Let us, therefore, perceive that the universal, living, conscious, intelligent Love you are is definitely a fulfillment of Purpose. It is the Universal All, fulfilling Its Purpose *as you* and *as your purpose.*

Does it appear to you that your daily activity and affairs are something far from, or different than, the fulfillment of a Universal Purpose? This could not be. You see, there are not two of you, one a Universal Identity and the other a human, limited identity. *You are One alone.* And no matter what your activity may be at the moment, it is the fulfillment of some essential Universal Purpose.

Every legitimate activity is the fulfillment of an infinite, inseparable Purpose. However, we must realize that *you are a specific Identity as well as being a Universal Identity.* Consequently, you have a specific Purpose to fulfill, as well as being the fulfillment of a Universal Purpose. The mistake has always been that it seemed that the distinct Identity was separate from, or other than, the inseparable Universal Identity. From this mistake stems the fallacy that the specific Identity must fulfill a purpose that is separate from, or other than, the Universal Purpose.

With the foregoing in mind, let us see just what exists as the Universal Purpose. Always be aware of the fact that your distinct fulfillment of Purpose can no more be separate from the Universal Purpose than can you—as conscious, living, intelligent Love—be separate from universal, conscious, living, intelligent Love.

You are one inseparable One, and your fulfillment of Purpose is one indivisible fulfillment of Purpose.

You see, the fulfillment of Purpose is evidenced as an infinite variety of distinct activities, even as the Universal All is evidenced as an infinite variety of distinct Identities. Never for one moment forget or doubt but that *your every activity is the universal Omniaction, and that It is fulfilling Itself as your distinct activity.*

As we stated before, the Universe—being Intelligence—must have an intelligent Purpose in being. It must eternally and constantly be the fulfillment of Its Purpose in being. The universal fulfillment of Purpose is eternal, constant Perfection. This means that the Universe must maintain Itself as ever-perfect, eternal, conscious, living, intelligent Love.

*This is the universal fulfillment of Purpose,* and every distinct fulfillment of Purpose is basically this universal fulfillment of Purpose revealed and evidenced as an infinite variety of specific fulfillments of Purpose. Thus, your distinct activity is inseparable from the Universal Purpose, which is the constant, eternal maintenance and sustenance of Itself as Absolute Perfection.

# Chapter VII

# Life Fulfills Its Purpose

Now we perceive the fact that the only fulfillment of Purpose must—of necessity—be the Universal All maintaining Itself as Absolute Perfection constantly and throughout eternity. Let us also perceive just how this Purpose is fulfilled in and as our normal daily activity and affairs. Let us perceive just how this Truth is evidenced, not only as our daily affairs but as our Body as well. We are to perceive just how Life, Mind, Consciousness, Love, are evidenced right here and now in and as *every* facet of our experience.

Right here, we must realize the inseparability of the living, conscious, intelligent Love that is God, and this realization must be maintained throughout all our contemplation.

Let us begin with Life. Let us see in what way we *seem* to limit Life Itself. As you know, Life is Activity. Thus, any illusion that appears to limit Life *seems* to manifest itself as a limitation of our activity. This fallacy presents itself in many ways. It is the Body that is predominantly considered as a manifestation of Life. Hence, let us first consider Life and Its fulfillment from the standpoint of the Body.

If Life seems to be increasingly limited, the Body also appears to become more limited in Its activity. Of course, this is entirely illusion; however, the fallacious picture does appear as a body that is more limited in its strength, freedom, and effortless activity. One of the most tragic of all illusions is the one called "old age." Oh, this is such a fallacy. If we did not know better, it would certainly sadden us to seemingly see these completely false pictures of age. Again and again, we hear someone say, "Oh, I used to be able to do these things, but I just can't seem to do them anymore." Right here is a false picture of Life. It misrepresents limitless Life and would have It appear to be limited in Its eternal, immutable, free activity. Its pretense is that Life is changing, losing Its strength, Its freedom, Its very purpose in being.

Sometimes we hear someone declare, "I just can't remember anything anymore, now that I am older." Oh my, that certainly is a falsehood about the eternal, changeless Mind. We could go on ad infinitum with these phantasmal reports. But let us go beyond these false statements and perceive just why these appearances—that are not genuine—continue to seem to be so real and so prevalent.

This entire fantasy called "old age," stems from the illusion that Life, Mind, Consciousness, Love, have a beginning. They are supposed to come into being, and they are supposed to go out of being. In the interim, they are supposed to mature, to weaken, to deteriorate, and finally to disappear. Now, that is certainly not a very joyous picture for any of us to consider. If it were true, there wouldn't be much purpose in being alive, and certainly there would be no joy in living. If we actually believe that Life, Mind, Consciousness, Love are born—begin—this fallacious misconception simply has to give way in the presence of eternal, living, conscious, intelligent Love. Nonetheless, this mistaken sense of Life will continue to seem to be genuine until its complete "nothingness" is perceived.

If living, conscious, intelligent Love ever entered a body, it would certainly mature and age in the body, and it also would someday die out of the body. But the fact is that living, conscious, intelligent Love is eternally Its own Substance, Its own Activity, and Its own Embodiment. How, then, can it enter the Body, mature or age in, or as the Body, and die out of the Body? *This is utterly impossible.* Life cannot die out of Itself. Consciousness cannot become unconscious of Itself. Mind cannot depart from Itself. Neither can Love desert Itself.

From the foregoing, you can see that it is all a misconception of that which constitutes the Body, and this explains why it seems to age and die. Of course, it is true that underlying this misconception is the illusion that there is a little, separate, personal life that can do something, know something, have something, or be something of itself.

Ah, right here is the crux of the whole illusion:

There is no separate person and no separate personal life that can do anything, know anything, have anything, or be anything of itself.

Once this fact is clearly and completely perceived, all the other fallacies of an altogether non-existent mind or identity are completely dissipated. Nothing they were, and nothing they remain.

Right here it is important to perceive the fact that *you* are never an illusion. Neither are you a deluded mind. An illusion is simply an illusion and nothing else. The only way an illusory fabrication could possibly exist would be if it could be accepted, believed, or imagined to be genuine. The illusion never actually deludes *you*. It is impossible that the conscious, perfect Mind that you are is the type of mind that could be deluded. The conscious, perfect Mind that you are is the very Mind that is God. And God is never deluded.

An illusion—nothingness—deludes only itself. It has nothing whatever to do with the Identity that you are. You know that an illusion is sheer nothingness. Genuinely, you are not aware of an illusion or of any of its delusions. In one of the prayers of *The Ultimate*, you will find the following: "How can I know what God knows not, when God is all that knows?"

Yes, it is impossible for the Mind that you are to know anything that is unknown to—and *as*—the Mind that is God. Therefore, you are not even cognizant of an illusion or of any of its delusions. In all our discussion of an illusion, please be aware of the fact that the Mind you are is completely unaware of an illusion and that this Mind is never deluded.

You are not alive as a little, temporary, illusory Life. You are not a separate identity or a separate, living, conscious mind. You never entered a temporary body, and neither were you ever alive in, or as, a temporary body. There is no such thing as Soul *and* Body. Soul and Consciousness are the same Essence. The Soul *is* the Body, and the Body *is* the Soul.

You do not inhabit a body. Rather, the conscious, living Mind you are constitutes the *only* Body you know or know your Self to be. If you could have entered a body, you could also have lived so many years in a body—to have inhabited it—and ultimately you would have to leave a body. And right here is where the fantasy called "time" enters the illusory picture. All the deceptive pictures of age, deterioration, birth, and death are based in the basic lie that there is such a thing as time.

*There is no time.* Some of the space scientists know that there is actually neither time nor space. Of course, they do not speak of it in this way because they know that it sounds "unreasonable," even ridiculous. Nevertheless, they are right. There really is neither time nor space. It is only an illusion that deceives itself into believing that time exists. You will recall that wonderful statement in our Bible:

The thing that hath been, it is that which shall be; and that which is done is that which shall be done: and there is no new thing under the sun" (Eccles. 1:9).

Right here is a statement of Absolute Truth. There *is no* time.

Every Truth, everything that is true, is eternally true. Every activity is an eternal activity. Nothing changes. Nothing is added, and nothing is ever subtracted from the infinite, eternal *Nowness* of constant Completeness.

An entire book could be written on the subject of this timeless, spaceless Universe and why it is completely devoid of either time or space. However, just now we must not diverge too much, lest we interfere with the continuity of our revelations. Suffice it to say that eternal, living, conscious, intelligent, perfect Mind is *now*.

Furthermore, this eternal Mind does not fulfill Its Purpose by being a temporal mind in a temporal body. Eternal Consciousness does not fulfill Its Purpose by being alive as a temporal body. *There is no such body.* That which appears to be a temporary body is simply an illusion's embodiment of itself. But this illusory formation is not the Body of you or me or of anyone. An illusion is not alive; it is not intelligent, neither is it conscious. It has no substance or activity. Being nothing, it has nothing, knows nothing, is nothing.

The realization that there is no time naturally means the perception that there is no time in which to be born, no time in which to mature, no time in which to deteriorate or age, and no time in which to die. There is no time that comprises an interim between birth and death, which means beginning and ending. There is no time in which to change. There is no time in which the body can become decrepit, inactive, sick, unwieldy, or abnormal in any way.

The eternal Body is as immutable as is the eternal Mind, Consciousness, Life, Love. This is true because the eternal Body is the eternal, immutable Mind, Life, Consciousness, Love. The living Body that you are can no more age than can the Universe deteriorate and age. The eternal Body you are can no more begin and end than can the Universe have beginning or ending. The eternal Body you are can no more suffer, be sick, aged, inactive, or decrepit than can the universal Body be—or become—any of these illusory fallacies.

The foregoing is true because the Life that is alive right now and here is universal, perfect, eternal Life. Timeless, changeless, ageless Life is the *only* Life that can be alive. It is the illusion called time that seems to limit man to just a certain number of years. It is this same illusion that seems to limit your perfect, free, purposeful activity to just a few short years. It is this same falsity that appears to limit your strength, your freedom, your harmony, and Perfection to a certain number of years.

Any illusion—lie—about anything has to give way before the fact—the Truth—that *is* that Thing. That which is true remains in Its Entirety forever. That which is false appears and has to disappear. Illusion makes its own so-called laws and is limited by these fallacious laws. Truth needs no laws. Truth is the Principle which is ever Self-governed, and thus It is Its own law. Any illusion, with all its false laws, passes, but Truth does not govern by laws, and neither does Truth pass away.

The illusion called time must, of necessity, end, as all illusion seems to begin and to end. In Revelation 1:3, we find a perfect statement of this Absolute Truth:

> Blessed is he that readeth, and they that hear the words of this prophecy, and keep those things which are written therein: for the time is at hand.

As stated in *The Ultimate*, this is no prophecy. Rather, it is a statement of the fact that all eternity, in Its completeness, exists this very moment. In illumined Consciousness, time is unknown and unknowable. Illumined Consciousness is aware of *only* that which is true. And, of course, there is no Consciousness that is not illumined, or enlightened Consciousness.

Universal Mind knows no limitations called time or space. Have you ever noticed that right along with this fallacy called old age, there also seems to be an increasing tendency to remain in an ever smaller circle? There is an apparent aversion to travel or to leave one's present environs.

It is in this way that the false limitations called space would, if possible, limit universal, living, conscious Mind. But where are the barriers? Where is there a circumference for Consciousness, Life, Mind, Love? Look at the sky and ask your Self this question: "Where does the Consciousness I am stop being conscious in this limitless Infinitude?" Can you draw a line of demarcation *between* you and the heavens?

Indeed, no line of demarcation encloses the universal, boundless, free Identity you are. As our friends the physicists now allege, time and space are the same thing, and they are beginning to realize that neither one of them exists as an actual absolute fact.

Now, where are the limitations? Where is the limitation that pretends that your health can be complete for just a limited number of years? Where is the limitation that can convince you that you are confined by either time or space? How can this limitation be, when there is neither time nor space?

Needless to say, from a little, limited, personal standpoint, there could be no realization of this glorious freedom. We simply cannot separate the boundless Life we are. This Life cannot be divided or separated into bits and parts of Itself. We cannot personalize the infinite, universal, impersonal All.

Beloved, the recognition of your boundless, free Identity is glorious. In this realization you are aware of being vibrant, dynamic, free, and oh, so joyous. There is an awareness of being surging, flowing, rhythmic Life. And it is in this way that you are the very conscious Presence of eternal, infinite Life fulfilling Its Purpose. This is the infinite, eternal Life that *you are*, fulfilling Its Purpose by being joyously, freely, harmoniously alive, eternally and infinitely, *as you.*

Eternity is *now*. Infinity is *here*. It is right here and right now that Life is fulfilling Its Purpose by being alive as you and as your Body. You and your Body are One. There is no other you, and there is no other body. Furthermore, you do not know anything about another you or about another body.

Do you wonder what all of the foregoing has to do with your daily living and experience? Truly, it has everything to do with your daily affairs. To live each day freely, joyously, and dynamically is indeed a wonderful fulfillment of the Purpose of Life in being. It is certainly a satisfying experience to be vibrantly, fearlessly alive, carrying on your activities, exulting in and as inexhaustible strength. If this Truth did not evidence Itself in and as our daily affairs, we might just doubt Its authenticity. But It does reveal Itself as Its own evidence of consistent, joyous, free, inexhaustible, undepletable living. Hence, It is practical within and as your daily life, your every activity, and as the activity of your Body.

# Chapter VIII

# Consciousness Fulfills Its Purpose

Life, Consciousness, Mind, Love — this, as we have said, is the Wholeness, the Allness, that is God. We have been discussing Life. We have said that Life has to be alive as Something. If Life were not revealed as living Substance, Life would be without evidence of Itself. A living Substance, or Essence, is requisite in order that Life may evidence Itself as the fulfillment of Its Purpose.

Of course, Life is alive as Its own Essence and activity. However, Life and Consciousness are inseparably One. Consciousness — Spirit, Soul — is a living Essence. Consciousness is alive. Life reveals Itself, evidences Itself, and fulfills Its Purpose by being alive as this Essence that we have called Spirit. Spirit is Consciousness. Soul is Consciousness. Consciousness is awareness of Being.

Life, actively aware of being All that Life is, evidences Itself as a Body comprised of Light, Life, Spirit, Soul, Consciousness. This, of course, is the Body of Light which is seen with the "eye that is single." When we see with, and *as*, the one Vision, we do see only the Body of Light. The single Vision is the only Vision. It is the illusion that *seems* to see solidity, density, darkness.

The Body of Light is that which has been called a spiritual Body. The Body of Light, Spirit, Consciousness is seen, known, and experienced. This Body is alive, and the living Essence that comprises this Body is forever perfect and eternal. Actually, *all that God is, is revealed and manifested as this glorious Body.* Just now, however, we shall continue with our consideration of living Consciousness evidenced as the Body of Light.

It is well, right here, to realize that conscious Life does not inhabit the Body. Conscious Life is not *in* the Body, as ink would be in a pen or water in a glass. Rather, conscious Life, living Consciousness, is the very Essence that exists *as* the Body.

Is it any wonder that the space fliers have discovered that the Body is weightless? The living Consciousness that is the Body has no awareness of weight. If this Body could be conscious of weight, it would, of necessity, be limited both in Its activity and in Its freedom.

When Jesus walked on the water and when he appeared within a room where the doors and windows were closed, did he appear as a Body of heavy, dark, dense, solid matter? Not at all. Jesus knew that there was no matter and no material body. He was not at all concerned with an illusory sense of body. Yet he appeared in and as a Body that was evident.

It was necessary that Jesus' Body be evident. Had it not been seen—yes, even touched and heard—

by the disciples and by all of those with whom He walked and talked, the Purpose of this living Consciousness would not have been fulfilled.

The Body must be evident. The Body is necessary to the complete fulfillment of the Purpose of living, conscious, intelligent Love. If this were not the Truth, no one would have seen the Body of Jesus walk on the water. Neither would they have seen the Body of Jesus in that room when the doors and windows were all closed.

Now, don't misunderstand these statements. We are not delving into spiritualism. This is not at all similar to what our friends the Spiritualists believe. It is entirely different, as all of us who perceive the pure Body of Light know. But we know what comprises the living Essence that is this Body, consisting of Spirit, Consciousness, Soul, Light.

All that comprises this Universe is God, Consciousness, aware of being what God is. All that comprises the infinite Identity is God, *conscious of all that God is.* Your Identity consists solely of *your awareness that you exist.* All there is of your Identity is your awareness of being all that you are.

God, this Universe, is complete. This means that the universal Consciousness is aware of being Everything and Everyone that is necessary to Its fulfillment of Its complete Purpose in being. This is why you are conscious of a Body. Actually, you are conscious *as* a Body. You are complete. The Body is necessary to your completeness. The Body is necessary to your complete fulfillment of Purpose. An identity without a body would be meaningless and would fulfill no purpose.

In order to be complete, God must evidence Itself as All that God is. God is the complete Evidence of Itself. In other words, God is Completeness as Itself and as Its Evidence of Itself. Therefore, you—your Identity—is complete. This means that the Body, which is necessary to your completeness, is essential to your complete Identity.

Furthermore, the Body is necessary to your complete fulfillment of Purpose. You wouldn't be the fulfillment of a very important Purpose if you were bodiless, would you? Of course not. Wasn't, and isn't, a Body necessary to the completeness of the one they called "Jesus"? Would his Purpose have been fulfilled if he had been bodiless? No!

Whatever is essential to your Completeness exists *as* the complete Identity that you are. Whatever is necessary to your complete fulfillment of Purpose exists within and *as* the complete, living, loving, conscious Mind that you are. A Body is necessary to your completeness and to your complete fulfillment of Purpose. Thus, the Body exists eternally within and as the eternal, living, intelligent, conscious Love that you eternally, constantly are.

Let us diverge for just a moment. It is the hope and one of the highest aspirations of some dedicated religious identities to completely obliterate the identity. They believe that the highest purpose is fulfilled when, or if, the identity can be completely dissolved in the One Infinite Identity.

Sometimes this Infinite Identity is called Nirvana. These are the ones who sincerely believe that the body is unnecessary and that it should be ostracized, or at least be ignored. Somehow, I have never been able to accept this belief. Even when I was supposed to be a child and was studying every religion I could discover, I always discarded or dismissed statements that suggested the obliteration of the Identity. Later, I became just as positive of the fact that the Body of each Identity was as eternal as was the Identity.

I am unwaveringly convinced that the eternal, conscious Identity forever exists *as* the eternal Body. This does not mean that the infinite, conscious Identity — You and every Identity in the Universe — is, or can be, confined to the Body or even to Its immediate environs. Rather, the Identity is unconfined and unconfinable. The complete fulfillment of Purpose of the Identity is as eternal as is the eternal Consciousness of Being that exists as the Identity. The Body is necessary to this complete fulfillment of Purpose. Thus, the eternality of the Body is essential to the eternal fulfillment of your Purpose in being. Perhaps a better way to state this Truth would be to say that it is in this way that God, the All, fulfills Its Purpose *as* the Identity you are.

Life is a Universal Constant. Thus, Life is a universally constant fact, or Truth. Life is a fact. It is true. Death is not a universal fact, thus is not true.

There really is no death. Even the very air is alive. If death could occur anywhere, it would have to occur everywhere. Whatever is true is true universally and eternally. If death could have ever taken place, the very Universe Itself would now be completely devoid of Life. In other words, there would be a dead Universe. Thus, there would be no Universe.

# Chapter IX

# Universal Purpose Fulfilled as Form

Life really is eternal and constant. It is never interrupted by either birth or death. However, as we have stated, Life has to be alive as Something. It is — and this Something is Everything that exists in or as Form.

Right here, we must make an unequivocal statement that may at first sound unreasonable, even ridiculous. Nonetheless, this statement must be made right here and now. There is no living, conscious, intelligent Love in existence that is devoid of Form. We will clarify this statement, and you will perceive why it is a statement of Absolute Truth. In order to do this, it is necessary to reveal just what constitutes Form.

Always the word *form* conjures up some picture of solidity and three-dimensional objects. But Form is much more than this fallacious misconception represents. However, we will begin our exploration of form from the standpoint of the physicists and then continue to the revelation that Form is not what it appears to be.

The physicists now say that the very air itself is comprised of structural atoms. Well, a structure is a form. Thus, according to their discovery, you can perceive that the air is constituted of Substance in form. You and I cannot see these structures. Yet the physicists have discovered that such forms exist.

The point here is that it is not at all important that we see the Essence in Form that constitutes this entire Universe. What is important is the fact that God, the Universe, exists in and *as* Form—everywhere, constantly, and eternally.

Now, you cannot imagine the structural atoms that comprise the air as being separated or divisible. Yet they exist as form. Right here let us be very sure that the atom is not what it appears to be. It is not matter. There really is no matter. Yet something that the physicists designate as the atom does exist, and it is genuine. The misconception of the substance and form of the atom cannot change the fact of the atom. Ultimately, everyone will know what constitutes this aspect of God called the atom. Thus, there will be no fear of it.

Did you know that form can be heard as well as seen? This is true, as is evidenced in music. Oh, yes, music does have form. The musicians even speak of music in terms of form. We know about the "three-part song form," the "sonata form," the "fugue form," etc. And there are many other forms in which music appears. Every musical composition has form.

In some advanced schools of music, the study of architecture is required, from the standpoint of architectural form. Then the students are required to perceive the fact that the various forms in which music appears are identically the same as the forms in which architecture appears. Right now, anyone trained in the art of musical composition can hear a composition of music and draw an outline of that composition that is a symbol for the form that he hears.

As stated before, this is a Universe of music. Music is omnipresent. Music is a Universal Constant, and It is an eternal Truth. All music is in form. The form is necessary to the completeness that is Music. The form is also necessary to the perfection, the harmony, and the rhythm of music. But it is well to realize that the form is necessary to the evidence of the fact that music exists. Music is one aspect of Universal Beauty. This Universal Beauty fulfills Its Purpose as perfect harmony, rhythm, and all that is required as Form.

Poetry has form. Poetry is sheer Beauty. It is noteworthy that many students of The Ultimate discover that they are poets, even though never before had they imagined that they could write in this specific medium. Many of these poems are sent to us here, and they are truly beautiful. Right here is the evidence that Beauty fulfills Its Purpose — not only as music but also as poetry. You will notice that Beauty fulfills Its Purpose in and *as* Form. Literature also has form. And the form of good literature is as perfect as is the form of good music or good poetry. From the foregoing, you can perceive that form is essential to the revelation and the evidence of Beauty.

Of course, you will understand that the *appearance* of solid substance in three-dimensional form is only the way we seem to see the actual Substance in Form that really does exist. Any architectural drawing, any outline of a musical composition is merely symbolic of the actual Essence, or Beauty, in Form that does exist. Nonetheless, that which has been revealed is sufficient to give us a hint of the Substance in Form, and the Form of the Substance, that seems to be invisible.

Our point in this entire presentation of form has been to reveal that all that is Substance exists in and as Form. It exists, and it does not matter whether the Form seems visible or even hearable. Only the trained composer or musician can discern the form in which music appears. Only the poet knows the form in which the poem is symbolized. Therefore, when we know what constitutes the Substance and the Form of the Body, we know what constitutes this Substance in Form that we call Body. Once we do know the true—and only—Nature of the Form and the Substance in Form called the Body, we are aware of that aspect of Beauty which exists as the Body.

Oh, yes indeed, the Body is beautiful. Remember, Beauty is a Universal Constant, and It fulfills Its Purpose by being beautiful. Hence, the Body could not exist if It were not Beauty in Form. Actually, everything is beautiful. Once you are aware of the infinite Beauty that is this Universe, you see Beauty in and as Everything. Thus, you *are* Beauty; you are what you see.

The notes on a page of music are not the music. They are merely symbols, signifying the fact that the music is present. In this same way, that which appears to be a body of matter is not the actual Substance in Form which is the Body. Rather, it is but a symbol, signifying the irrevocable fact that the Body, consisting of living, intelligent, loving Consciousness, is here.

This does not mean that you have two bodies. That which *appears* to be matter in form is not a body at all. The composer hears the music before ever the notes—symbols—are written. Thus, the music can be heard whether or not there are any notes or symbols in view.

In like manner, it is possible to see the genuine and only actual Body, whether or not the symbolic appearance of body is in view. But, oh my, let us never mistake the symbol for the genuine Body that does exist right here and now. The symbol of itself is nothing. If there were no actual Body, there could be no symbol.

Sometimes it has seemed that we were so aware of the symbol that we did not perceive the actuality that it symbolized. The symbol can even seem to obstruct our vision and thus obliterate our awareness of the genuine Body of living Light. That which appears to be a body of matter can appear to obstruct our awareness of the Body that consists of living, conscious Mind. Yet matter of itself is nothing but illusion. Thus, it cannot really obstruct Mind, Consciousness, Life Itself. Illusion has no substance.

Notes may be erased. They may be consigned to the trash heap or to the furnace. Yet this has nothing to do with the fact that the Music remains. Nothing can destroy the Body of the composition. In this same way, the symbol which appears to be a body of matter may seem to be erased, but the Body remains forever the same. Nothing can injure, harm, change, or destroy this beautiful evidence of Beauty in Form.

Now, here is a paradox. When the genuine and only Body is perceived and experienced, that which appears to be a body of density begins to take on a better appearance. Our friends tell us that we are looking younger, getting more beautiful, appearing more vital, or that our skin is more glowing. This is the way it appears to them. But we know better. We know it is only that the eternal, perfect, beautiful, immutable Body of Light is becoming more and more apparent so that it is seen ever more perfectly, even by the vision that appears to view it from the standpoint of the symbol. It is all a matter of Consciousness because Consciousness is the Essence in Form that comprises this eternal Body.

We have said that Life is a Universal Constant. Well, this means that Consciousness is also a Universal Constant. Life has to be conscious in order to be alive. In this same manner, Consciousness has to be alive in order to be conscious. From this you can see that this Universe, and all that exists as the infinite variety in Form that comprises It, consists of Life that is conscious and Consciousness that is alive.

The foregoing statement of Absolute Truth will bear much contemplation. When its Truth is fully perceived, you will discover that you *are* the universal, living Consciousness, the Universal Consciousness that is eternally and constantly alive. Furthermore, you will also perceive the wonderful fact that the Substance in Form, Body, that you are, consists of this very same universal, eternal, constant, living Consciousness.

It is in this discovery that you will realize the entire fallacy of a born body, which you inhabit for a while and from which you must be ejected, or make your escape. You never entered the eternal Body that consists of eternal, conscious Life. Neither can you ever depart from this ever-perfect, beautiful Body. Never have you inhabited this Body. On the contrary, this Body has always existed as your own forever living Consciousness, and you will ever exist as this same imperishable Substance. You never entered your Self. You do not inhabit your Self, and you can never leave your Self. Your Self is the forever living Consciousness that you are. And this ever living conscious Self is the Body you are.

Conscious Life fulfills Its Purpose by being *consciously* alive. But the Consciousness that is alive, and knows Itself to be alive, is the Substance in

Form of the Body. This conscious, living Substance can be aware of nothing other than Itself. Being eternal and constant, It can have no awareness of beginning or ending. Neither can It be aware of any interruption of Its consciousness—Its awareness—of being. Conscious Life, or living Consciousness, is never interrupted by unconsciousness. It has no awareness of anything that can interrupt It or interfere with It. Indeed, there is nothing existing that can obstruct, interfere with, or even oppose conscious Life.

Of course, you realize that we are dwelling at quite some length on that aspect of your being which is the Body. This is rather important because it is an absolute necessity for all of us to perceive and experience the eternal Body, forever perfect, that knows Itself to consist of conscious, living, intelligent Love. Most of our difficulties seem to be based in a misconception of Body, Once we know and experience the evidence of being the eternal, perfect, changeless Body of Light, we can, for the most part, forget it. In fact, the Body does not constantly call attention to Itself once we are aware of Its genuine Nature.

All of us know that the illusory, or symbolic body seems to make many demands upon us. It is almost constantly intruding its fallacious claims upon our attention. When we are fully aware of the universal nature of the conscious Life that constitutes the Body, It—the Body—no longer seems to be so important. We are not concerned with the Body as Body. Rather, we know that the Consciousness we are is aware of Its perfection *as* Body, and we do not "feature" it so much. Only when we are engaged in our daily tasks of cleanliness, neatness, or the dressing of It are we really aware of the Body. Generally, It does not intrude into our awareness of being. But in order to realize and evidence this bodily freedom, it is necessary to clearly understand what constitutes the Body.

We have stated that Consciousness is your awareness that you exist. Consciousness can only be aware of that which does exist. That which does exist is that which is true. Consciousness cannot be aware of anything that is not true because It can have no awareness of anything that does not exist. That which is not true does not exist. Even the All that is God could not know something that has no existence. And you are the living Consciousness which is God, Life, aware of Being.

It is not our intention to overemphasize the Body. But we know that a clear perception of the Body—and Its activities—is essential because apparently there are very few who consciously perceive and experience being the eternal, perfect Body of living Consciousness. And until we do experience *being* this perfect, changeless, eternal Body, we are going to seem to go right on with this appearance of birth, maturity, deterioration, age, and finally, death,

Furthermore, this clear perception of being is necessary if we are to be through with this "no thing" of sickness and sin. Oh, yes, it is the Body that seems to sin. However, we must never forget that both sickness and sin are thoroughly mythical, and a body that can deteriorate, age, etc., is as nonexistent as is a body that can sin.

Jesus is reported to have asked, "Which of you convinceth me of sin?" (John 8:46). He asked this deeply penetrative question because he knew that there was neither a mind nor a body capable of sinning. He knew the complete fallaciousness of the entire illusory pictures. We do not dwell upon the nothingness called a sinner or sin. Rather, we remain ever more aware of pure, conscious, living Mind, to whom sin or a sinner is unknown. I have never known anyone to be helped by regarding him as a sinner.

We freely accept the fact that Consciousness exists eternally. Anything that eternally exists has to be perfect. This is true because we know that any appearance of imperfection presages the end of that which appears to be, or to become, imperfect. Thus, eternal Consciousness is forever perfect. Consciousness can only be aware of what It is, so Consciousness can only be aware of Perfection. Hence, there is no awareness of imperfection.

Now, bear in Mind the fact that we are speaking of the Substance which comprises your Body. This is true because Consciousness is the *only* Substance in existence. Conscious Perfection *is*. Conscious imperfection *is not*. Conscious Perfection is All. All is conscious Perfection. Perfection is the only Presence, thus, All that is present.

Only that which is present has, or is, Power. Perfection is the only Presence; thus, Perfection is the only Power. Perfection reigns supreme. It is omnipotent because It is Omnipotence. Perfection is a universal fact. It is also a Universal Constant. Perfection is omnipresent because It is Omnipresence.

When Jesus apparently quieted the storm, saying, "Peace, be still," he knew that he was not dispelling or casting out a storm. Rather, he was conscious of the Allness, the *oneness*, of that which was, and is, present. He knew that the very presence of Universal Love, Joy, and Peace precluded the possibility of the presence of any threat to Life, Mind, Consciousness. In other words, Jesus knew what was present. And thus, he was not concerned with what was not present. He also knew that only that which was present was Power. Perfection was, and is, ever present. Thus, there can never be a storm or anything that appears to be destructive.

This is our "Peace, be still," to everything that would seem to be destructive, whether it be a threat to Life or to Joy, Peace, Abundance, or whatever; we, too, can say, "Peace, be still," and that which is present—thus, omnipotent—will be evidenced.

We *are* the Mind that was in Christ Jesus, for there is no other mind for us to be. Thus, we know just what he knew, and knows. Our "Peace, be still" is our knowledge—our awareness—that Perfection alone is present; Perfection alone is power; Perfection alone reigns. Of course, this is only another way of saying, "God is All; All is God."

God, Perfection, being the only Mind, there isn't any mind that knows itself to be imperfect. Therefore, imperfection is actually unknown. Truly, there isn't any consciousness that is aware of being painful, swollen, or infected. There isn't any consciousness that is aware of being diseased, ill, old, uncomfortable, or troublesome in any way. There isn't any consciousness that is aware of being the substance or the activity of an abnormal growth called a tumor or a malignancy. There isn't any consciousness that knows itself to be abnormal or imperfect in any way. There isn't any consciousness that is aware of aging, of deteriorating, or of becoming decrepit.

You see, the Consciousness that knows anything —that knows Existence—is the Substance, the Intelligence, and the Life of that Existence. Again and again, we have said, "I know what I am; I am what I know." And this is a profound Truth.

This Truth should be contemplated frequently. A full revelation of the tremendous Truth revealed in this statement will mean glorious experiences of joy, peace, and perfection. This is the true significance of the statement "I AM THAT I AM." When we understand the wonderful significance of this statement,

91

we can, and do, perceive and evidence the omnipotence of the Truth it signifies. As the meaning of this statement becomes apparent, we can confidently say:

> I am that which I see. I am that which I know. I am that which I experience. I am that which I evidence. I am the Substance, the Activity, and the Form of All that I see, hear, sense, feel, or experience. I am All of this because I am that I AM. I am All of this because I know what I am, and I am what I know.

This Universe consists entirely of God, aware of being All that God knows. God, the Universe, fulfills His—or Its—Purpose in being by *being* All that God knows. Your Universe consists entirely of you, aware of being All that you know. You fulfill your Purpose in being by *being* All that you know. There is nothing in or as your Universe, your experience, or your Body that does not consist of the Consciousness that you are, aware of being All the Truth you know.

There is a chapter in our textbook, *The Ultimate*, entitled "Seeing Is Being." If you will again read this chapter, you will discover far greater significance in it than you have hitherto realized. Seeing *is* Being, and the Being and the seeing are identical. To *see* means to *perceive*. It is Consciousness that perceives, but the Consciousness that perceives *is the entire Essence and Activity of that which It perceives.* It is in this way that God, Consciousness, fulfills Its Purpose by *being* the Consciousness that you are.

Beloved one, do you realize that you are absolutely necessary to God's fulfillment of His Purpose in being? We find it easy to perceive that God is necessary to our existence, our completeness, our fulfillment of Purpose, but most of us find it a little more difficult to realize that we are necessary to the Completeness and the complete fulfillment of Purpose which is God. Nonetheless, this is true. If you did not exist, God would not be complete. If your Purpose in being were not fulfilled, and eternally fulfilled, God's Purpose would not be completely and eternally fulfilled.

You see, there is no separation between the infinite Purpose and the specific Purpose because God is one indivisible, eternal, constant fulfillment of Purpose. Yet each and every Identity in existence is essential to the complete fulfillment of Purpose which is God, conscious of being what God knows and is.

Where we seem to get into trouble is when we falsely assume that we have some little, separate purpose of our own to fulfill. It is as though a drop of water in the wave of the ocean should imagine that it could fulfill its purpose by turning and going against the ceaseless motion of the wave. Is it any wonder that we seem to encounter so many difficulties, when we imagine that we have some separate purpose of our own that we must fulfill? Indeed, no. The marvel is that we don't seem to get into greater difficulties than we seem to encounter every day.

Now, you may wonder just how you are going
to know whether your existence, your normal daily
activity, is God fulfilling Its Purpose as your fulfillment
of Purpose, or whether you are attempting to fulfill
some separate purpose of your own. You can be—
and are—aware of this distinction by the realization
of your indivisible Universal Nature. But there are
other ways in which you can be aware of the
distinction between an *apparent* fulfillment of purposes
and the genuine and only fulfillment of Purpose.

There are many statements in our Bible that
exemplify the Infinite *I* as the fulfillment of Its Purpose
by being the specific "I." But we shall mention but two
of the more outstanding statements.

> But Jesus answered them, My Father worketh
> hitherto, and I work (John 5:17).

Jesus well knew that the *I* that acts, that fulfills
Its Purpose, is the "I" that we are, fulfilling each
specific Purpose. The following quotation is proof
that this knowledge was not reserved for Jesus
alone.

> For it is God which worketh in you both to
> will and to do of his good pleasure (Phil. 2:13).

In the first of the foregoing statements, we find
Jesus definitely saying that because God was eternally
"working," fulfilling His Purpose, he—Jesus—was
fulfilling his Purpose.

And in the second statement, Paul reveals that
this great Truth is equally true as each and every

one of us. Here Paul was writing to the Philippians, and in this epistle he made clear the fact that it was God who worked in, and as, the Philippians, and it was God who was fulfilling *His* Purpose as *their* Purpose. Paul also made it clear that it was God's good pleasure to fulfill His Purpose in being *as* their fulfillment of Purpose.

Now, we can perceive that the Truth which was, and is, true of Jesus and the Philippians is also true as you, as the *I* that I am and as the *I* that evidences Itself as Everyone. True it is that most of us do not appear to be cognizant of this fact. Yet it is true, even though we may seem, for a little moment in our eternal Being, to be unaware of this great Truth.

Indeed, it is possible for us to know whether or not our activity is the fulfillment of an infinite Purpose as well as being the fulfillment of a specific Purpose. For instance, sometimes we "feel" a strong impulse, even an urge, to act in a certain way. Perhaps it may be nothing more than an urge to write a letter or to make a telephone call. It may be that we feel impelled to buy or to sell a certain item. It may be that we feel it is very important—although we may not know exactly why—for us to make a major move of some kind or to change our employment or any number of activities that had hitherto been acceptable but now there is an indication that they are unacceptable.

We need not question these impulses. But we should, by all means, let them "percolate" within and as our Consciousness. As we remain a full openness, we find that the entire Purpose and Its fulfillment is clear and exceedingly apparent. When this takes place, we have no choice. It is not that we have chosen to act. Rather, it is that God, the Universal All, chooses to fulfill His Purpose within and as each Identity.

Now, lest there be some misunderstanding here, let us point out a salient fact: there is no God outside of or other than your own Consciousness that chooses to *be* you or that chooses to act as your activity. The Universal God is the Christ-Consciousness that you are. Hence, you are constantly, eternally aware of what to do, how to act, when to act, what to say, and when to say it. Jesus was well aware of this fact:

> Ye have not chosen me, but I have chosen you, and ordained you, that ye should go and bring forth fruit, and that your fruit should remain; that whatsoever ye shall ask of the Father in my name, he may give it you (John 15:16).

God is the Christ, even as the Christ is God. The Christ-Consciousness is the Presence of the Consciousness that is God. And it is this Christ-Consciousness that fulfills Itself by being the Christ right here and now as every one of us. Therefore, in the foregoing statement of Jesus, he was simply referring those whom he was addressing to their own Christ-Consciousness. To "ask" in this sense means to acknowledge the Presence of God in the

Name of the Christhood—which is the Self. And Jesus assures us that this kind of asking will bring forth fruitage. In other words, recognizing our God—Christ—Nature, we will certainly complete the fulfillment of Purpose that is God's Purpose in being us and our Purpose in being the Christ which is God.

I have gone into this subject quite thoroughly because the word *specific* can seem to be misunderstood. It can appear to have a connotation of separateness or otherness. And of course, nothing could be further from the Truth.

For instance, a wave of the ocean *is that* specific wave; a drop of water *is* that specific drop of water; but the wave is inseparable from the ocean, and the drop of water is inseparable from the wave. This is true because the wave, as well as the drop of water, *is* the ocean, even as the ocean *is* the wave. But the ocean is also the drop of water. It is all ocean. It is all water. No separation, no division, no "otherness."

In the second volume of this classwork, *Fulfillment of Purpose*, you will find many specific similes and specific instances of the way in which the universal fulfillment of Purpose is evidenced in, through, and *as* your specific daily activity. Before you read and contemplate the Truths revealed in the second volume of this classwork, it is well for you to be firmly convinced of the indivisibility of all Essence, all Activity, all fulfillment of Purpose.

For now, suffice it to realize that never for one moment should we depart from the basic fact that this Universe, Its fulfillment of Purpose, whether universal or specific, is one inseparable, integral Entirety, Whole, All. It is impossible to stress too powerfully the importance of maintaining our awareness of the indivisibility of the All. This is true because all our seeming difficulty stems from the illusion of separateness, otherness, which, of course, is duality.

# Chapter X

## Being Versus Possessing

Sometimes it seems that there are some words that could very well be omitted from our vocabulary. Among these words are *your*, *mine*, or *my*. It is true that we constantly use these words. We speak of "my" house, "my" trees or roses. Also we often speak of "my" body or of "your" body. This is all right so long as we remain aware of our inseparable Essence and Activity. But if we are not very alert, we can easily fall into the trap of separation and dualism. Let us be on guard in this matter.

Although the words of themselves are not of such great importance, our consciousness of what these words mean to us is of vital importance. Whenever we use, read, or hear a word that ordinarily denotes possession, we will realize that possession of itself is a falsity.

There is a vast distinction between *being* something and possessing something. To possess means to have. To have means twoness. It means to own or to possess something that belongs to you as a separate individual. Thus, it means duality. No one can "have" himself. No one can "possess" himself. One can only *be* Himself.

If we could possess anything, it would have to be but a temporary possession. It would have to be something separate from us that we had acquired. There is nothing that we can add to our Self. There is nothing that we can subtract from our Self. We are eternally and constantly complete, and this Completeness that we *are* can never be augmented or depleted. There can never be anything true of or as us that is not true as God. Nothing can ever be added to God. Nothing can ever be taken from God. This, beloved, is why nothing can ever be added to or taken from *you*.

There is nothing separate from us that we can acquire. There is nothing separate from us that we can lose or that can remove itself from us. In this way, there is nothing that ever enters into us or that ever departs from us.

To possess anything would mean to separate the infinite, inseparable All. It would mean to separate the inseparable Essence, Consciousness, Mind, Life, Love that we are. It would have to mean that the Infinite Inseparable had separated Itself into bits and parts of Itself. We do not possess anything. How can we? Why should we possess anything? Aren't we Everything?

We do not possess Intelligence, yet we are intelligent. This is true because we are Mind Itself. This fact explains why we simply cannot act unintelligently. This is why we always know what to do, how to act, and this is why we always act intelligently. Knowing this Truth, we simply cannot make a mistake. Knowing that Intelligence is a universal, eternal Constant and knowing that *we* are this Universal Constant, we also know that there can be no lapse in the Intelligence that we are. There can be no vacuum in the eternal, universal, constant Intelligence that we are. It is impossible for us to lapse from ourselves. It is impossible that we could be a vacuum within and as ourselves. Never can we lapse or depart from the universal—yet specific—perfect, conscious Mind that we are.

All that we are saying here is absolutely true. It is Absolute Truth. It is true whether or not we seem to be aware of the fact that it is true. However, it does not help us very much unless we know it to be true and unless we know that *we are this Truth Itself.* It is necessary to realize that we know this Truth. But of greater importance is the necessity to know that we *are* this Truth. Again, let us repeat: "I know what I am; I am what I know."

Apparently there are those who falsely believe that they can acquire or attain power. There are also those who are deceived by the illusion that they possess power. Once they are deluded in this way, the illusion always seems to crave more and more power. Then, too, it is always fearful that its power will be lessened or that it will be dispossessed of its illusory power. But "power belongeth unto God" alone.

Nonetheless, it is this false assumption — that "man with breath in his nostrils" can possess power — that engenders the world illusion of trouble, bondage, hatred, and war. The fallacious sense that man can possess power always has its roots in the completely phantasmic little "I" or ego. Always this illusory claim evidences itself as a greatly inflated, although completely false, ego. It is this pseudo little "I" that imagines it is a great leader and that demands strict obedience to its dictates.

Actually, this is a false picture of "nothing." No man can possess power. You see, if anyone could possess power, he could also use this power or misuse it. This would give him power, for good or for evil, over those he considered as "others."

Yes, there does seem to be an ever-increasing determination by certain misled so-called leaders to completely dominate all nations and peoples. But Mind, Consciousness, Life, Love is All, and this Entirety is indivisible. Who, then, are these other people? What, then, are these other nations? They are only figments of an illusory "nothingness" called the mind of man. But there really is no such man.

There will come a day when the world will realize that it is completely free of these despots. When it is clearly realized that God is the Universe, the Earth Planet, and all that comprises Totality, the assumptive dictators of the world will no longer even *appear* to exist.

Universal, living Mind does not crave power. This Mind does not even use power. Only in the sense that God *is* all Power, does Power belong to God. But this Omnipotence is not power over anyone or anything. Being inseparably All, It is simply the Power of *being*. God, infinite Mind, is the Power of seeing, perceiving, being. Omnipotence is all Power. It is omnipresent constantly and universally, and It is eternal. Above all, It is indivisible and equally present everywhere and forever. This, beloved, is the Power of *Being*.

We know that we are just what God is and nothing else. This is true because there is nothing else for us to be. Hence, we know that we are the only Power. We also know that we are the Power of seeing, perceiving, and being that which we see. We do not see any nations or peoples outside of, or other than, our Self. Thus, we know that everyone we see is the very same Power that we are and that actually this Power is not invested in any little personal "I."

That which God is, we are. That which God is not, we cannot be. Since God is the Power of perceiving, thus the Power of Being, it follows that we also are only the Power of perceiving, thus the Power of Being. Hence, we do not use the infinite Power that we are. We do not *have* power. Yet we *are* Universal Power Itself. The Power that we are is not a power over anyone or anything. Rather, it is the universal, indivisible Omnipotence that is *All Power*.

It is only the illusory sense of power that makes it *seem* that there is a power that can be used to dominate or to enslave those called "others."

When we are consciously in illumination, we are aware of seeing and being this universal, impersonal Power. But always there is this great surge of Oneness, of Love. It is in this glorious experience that we perceive nothing that is separate or other than our Self. There are no "others." There is nothing "other" than the inseparable One that we are. Thus, there is nothing, and no one, over which we can exert power or use the Power that we are in any way.

Do not be deceived about this wonderful word *Power*. Power without Love would indeed be an evil thing. But Omnipotence is Love, for Omnipotence is God and God is Love. Without Love, there could be no Power. It is in this awareness that we perceive that we really are omnipotent Love. And it would never occur to us that we could possess or use the Universal Power of Love that we are.

Now we can joyously say:

I do not possess Intelligence, yet I am supremely intelligent, for I am infinite, Universal Mind. I am the supreme, all-knowing Intelligence which is all knowledge. I do not possess Perfection, yet I am completely perfect because I am infinite, complete Perfection. I do not possess Power, yet I am infinitely powerful because I am the very Presence of Universal Omnipotence.

I do not possess Life, yet I am alive because I am eternal, constant, uninterrupted Life. I do not possess Consciousness, yet I am conscious, for I am infinite, eternal Consciousness. I do not possess Love, yet I am forever loving, for I am infinite, eternal Love. I do not possess Supply, yet I am eternally and constantly supplied, for I am infinite, omnipresent Supply.

I am the Substance and the Form of all that I could ever appear to need. I am my own Completeness; all that is necessary to my eternal completeness, I am right here and right now. It is not that I have anything; rather, it is that I *am* Everything. I am complete Health, Wholeness, Vitality because I am that I AM.

I am complete Knowledge because I am infinite, eternal Mind. I am complete perception because I am Universal Consciousness. All that God is, I am. This is my only perception. Thus, this is my only Being. I *know* what I am; I *am* what I know.

Oh, beloved One, it is all a matter of Consciousness. To perceive is an *act* of Consciousness. Perception is Consciousness in action, and this activity is Omniaction, or God in action. Really, there is nothing other than Consciousness. We cannot stress too strongly the importance of knowing the omnipotent Omnipresence that is Consciousness. Whenever an instantaneous perception of Perfection is evidenced, it is always a sudden awareness, Consciousness, of the Perfection we eternally are. That which is called a miracle is always present. It is simply omnipresent Perfection consciously perceived and evidenced.

It seems that our entire training in the illusory world of man "with breath in his nostrils" is directed toward "doing" something, "attaining" something, "gaining" something, etc. Indeed, it is no small thing to perceive the fallacy of this miasmic training. But it is even a greater marvel that we are capable of canceling this false training from our entire experience. Many students of the Ultimate are living freely, joyously, and without effort through the perception that Consciousness does not attain, neither does It possess. It simply *is*—right here and now—all that It could possibly seem to need or to desire.

Needless to say, this perception cannot be "attained" through thinking. The so-called mind that thinks, that reasons, or that concentrates, belongs in the category of illusion or nothingness. Its seeming activity can only appear to conceal the Perfection, the infinite Abundance, that is already present.

It is true that sometimes it seems almost impossible to quiet the so-called thinking mind. But the so-called human mind cannot be silenced by any assumptive mental effort. You see, the pseudo mind that tries to quiet an assumptive mind is nothing more or less than this same illusory mind, trying to quiet itself. Therefore, something greater, more profound, has to be experienced. It is not a matter of doing something to quiet the so-called thinking mind. Rather, it is a matter of "letting go." It is an effortless awareness of simply "being." No one can think himself into being. We can only be conscious of being. And this awareness of *being* is experienced when we are no longer trying to do something in order to become that which we eternally are.

Right here is where metaphysics is transcended, and the Absolute is revealed. All of us have been through the metaphysical way of trying to do something, accomplish something, or attain something. Now it is necessary that we completely dispel this fallacious way. And perhaps those of us who have been through the metaphysical schools find this is the most difficult of all to realize. Difficult it is; yet it is not impossible, as many students know.

The machinations of the assumptive mind are indeed subtle, and it is well to be ever alert to this subtlety. For instance, we may believe that we are all through with delusion, and suddenly we will find that we are reading Truth with some desire to attain or to accomplish some objective. Sometimes we may even imagine that if we can only understand the Truth in some article or book, we will become enlightened and thus be freed of some seeming difficulty. Right here is one of the most subtle of all of the illusory arguments of doing, accomplishing, attaining. Never should we read any statements of Truth with any object in mind. Always our reading should be for the sheer joy of seeing, perceiving, and being.

There are innumerable ways in which this subtle deception can appear to creep into our reading and even our contemplation. Sometimes the desire to experience illumination is so strong that it may seem to obstruct this glorious experience. This is particularly true if we imagine that illumination may bring about a so-called healing. There appears to be a conviction that if only we could experience illumination, all our troubles would be over. This is but one prong of a two-pronged illusion. Above all, we must perceive that the illusion of itself is nothing. There is no deluded mind. There is only one Mind, and this Mind is never deluded.

The seeming desire to *become* the Perfection that we already are is one prong of the above mentioned illusion. The second prong of this illusion is that we must experience illumination in order to consciously *be* or *become* the Perfection that we already are. Neither of these fantasies has any basis in fact, and they certainly can seem to delay our conscious perception of that perfect, free Entirety which we are.

You see, the desire to become illumined is based in the fallacy that we are not already illumined Consciousness. Really, *there is no one who is not illumined Consciousness.* No one could be conscious unless he existed as the Consciousness that is God. There are not two consciousnesses. Therefore, the Consciousness that is God is the Consciousness that you are, that I am, and that everyone actually is.

This being true, it follows that everyone who is conscious of being, of existing, is illumined Consciousness. In our book, *You Are the Splendor*, we discover that everyone does consciously experience some aspect of illumination. From the foregoing fact, it is evident that everyone is illumined — enlightened — Consciousness.

Even though it seems that these experiences of illumination are not understood and that they only occur occasionally, they could not possibly take place unless the Consciousness of the experiencer *were* illumined Consciousness. It is simply as though this glorious, Universal Consciousness broke through the clouds from time to time, revealing Itself as the only Self in all Its glory. But this illumined Consciousness does not come and go. It is constantly present as the Consciousness of each one of us, and it is because It is present that It does sometimes disperse the seeming clouds of darkness or ignorance.

Now, of course, we must go further with this revelation. We must realize the nothingness of a mind or consciousness that is ignorant. As there is but one Mind, there simply cannot be a mind that is ignorant. Thus, even the seeming "clouds of ignorance" must be dispelled.

We can only know that we exist because we are conscious. There is nothing that can be conscious other than Consciousness. The only Consciousness that is conscious is illumined, or enlightened, Consciousness. This being true, it is inevitable that our Consciousness that we exist is illumined, or enlightened, Consciousness, aware of being. Our only awareness of being is our Consciousness, being the Light. *All really is Light.* Therefore, our only Consciousness that we exist is our awareness of being the Light in which there is no darkness at all.

All that is ever necessary for us is to recognize this profound Truth. It is our recognition and our full and complete acceptance of this Truth that constitutes our only actual Consciousness of being. If we must still seem to think, let us "think on these things." Let us not think on the darkness—the ignorance—which we are not. Let us think on the Light, the complete, all-intelligent Mind which we are. Nonetheless, the so-called thinking mind is entirely mythical. Mind does not think. It *knows.* And this eternal, constant knowledge is Consciousness. In and as Consciousness, there is no arriving, no coming, and no going. We simply *are,* and we are aware of *being* what we are.

Now, you may wonder what all of this has to do with the subject of this chapter, which is "Being versus Possessing." Beloved, it has everything to do with it. This is true because it is the *being* which takes away all the struggle of seemingly *becoming.* It is the conscious being that takes away all the fallacious effort of attainment, of accomplishing, or of possessing anything. All we could ever possess would have to be our Self. And, of course, the Self is forever Self-possessed. But this is not an acquired possession. Rather, it is an inevitable consequence of the fact of Being.

Beloved, I know that the foregoing requires much consideration. Don't strive to understand it. The enlightened Consciousness that you are *already understands it* because It knows what It eternally is. If you can, this moment, accept the fact that this is true and that *this is you*, there will be no seeming struggle. There is much more to be read between the lines here than the words can convey. Just let it reveal itself effortlessly.

Since you are reading these words, it is inevitable that the full and complete perception is right here and now ready to be realized. Let it be. It already *is*. Nothing can stop that which already *is* from being. Of one thing you can be sure: full comprehension of the Truth of the foregoing statements will mean that there is no more struggle, no more attempt to attain or to become that which you are, right here and right now.

This revelation obliterates all the strain from our everyday experience. However, we are not inactive. On the contrary, we are intensely active. It cannot exactly be said in words. But our sense of being active is more keen than any we have ever known. Yet there is no false sense of strain or of "trying." It is simply an awareness of being. But oh, what an effortlessly *active* sense of being! We know that we cannot "get" anything. We know that we cannot attain anything. We know that we cannot accomplish anything. We know that we cannot possess any-thing. We even know that we cannot fulfill *any* purpose of ourselves.

We are so unaccustomed to realizing our eternal, selfless Being that, just at first, the foregoing statements may present a false picture of inactivity, indolence, purposelessness, or even of boredom. Nothing could be further from the Truth. Please be assured that there is nothing static, nothing unin-teresting, and nothing boring about this normal way of Life. Rather, there is a constant, intense, active interest in just observing the glorious, free activity which constantly goes on as the fulfillment of purpose which we eternally are.

In the second volume of this classwork, you will discover the way in which this activity functions in your daily affairs. However, if you are to experience being the glorious Truths revealed in this second volume, it is necessary for you to first comprehend the Truths herein revealed. Please be assured that there is nothing impractical in this revelation. On the contrary, it is the most normal, and thus the most practical, way of Life we have ever experienced. It is just that all the effort, all the struggle, the uncertainty, frustration, and strain no longer seem to plague us.

This Life is a glorious, free, joyous experience. Heaven is perceived to be Earth, and Earth is perceived to be heaven. Of course, eternally it has been this way. Earth and heaven have always been one inseparable Entirety. But it has seemed as though—for a little split-second in the eternity of our being—we have been unaware of this fact. But never mind, the Light is shining *now*. Nothing can stop it because the Light is all there is, and there is nothing in existence that can stop the Light from being the Allness, the Entirety, that It eternally and constantly is.

Now it is clear why there can be no struggle, strife, or strain in our normal daily affairs. No longer does it seem to us that we are trying to get anything. We are not concerned about our so-called possessions. On the contrary, we realize that we can thoroughly enjoy all the beauty, all the good, all the abundance without any lurking fear that we may someday be deprived of them.

No one imagines that he or she can possess a beautiful sunset or sunrise. Yet all of us may freely enjoy this Beauty. In the enjoyment and appreciation of Beauty, there is one all-important fact for us to recognize: we have to *be* Beauty in order to see it. It has been said that "Beauty is in the eye of the beholder." Certain it is that in order to "see" or to "hear" Beauty, we must be conscious of It.

Our Consciousness comprises everything and everyone that we see or hear. Consciousness comprises everything that we know. Thus, because our Consciousness is Beauty, we must ever be aware of It. This we realize fully when we are aware of *being* everything, rather than having or possessing anything. In this way, we enjoy the Beauty—which is all there is—in the same free way we enjoy the Beauty of a sunrise or sunset, hear beautiful music, etc.

Sometimes the illusion of ownership seems to present problems. Perhaps we are deluded by fear of loss. Illusion may argue that we may lose our so-called possessions. Oh, there are many ways in which we can appear to be worried by what we consider to be our possessions.

For instance, we may seem to fear that our investments may become valueless, our stocks depreciate, our property decrease in value or be overtaxed. Oh yes, illusory fear may argue that some valued "possession" may be stolen from us. These are just a few of the innumerable problems that accompany the illusion that we can really possess anything.

# Chapter XI

# Supply Reinterpreted

Of course, in the foregoing statements, it may *appear* that we are speaking of something material — money — which we invest in another something that is material, called "things." We have often stated, "There is no matter." So this activity is never what it appears to be. There is, however, a spiritual fact that is signified by these so-called human investments. Money is not material. The things in which we invest are not material. All that *seems* to be material is but an appearance which symbolizes the Presence of Spirit, Consciousness, as that aspect of Itself. Supply, symbolized by the appearance called "money" and "things," may be compared to the note on the sheet of music. It symbolizes the tone, yet never is it the actual tone. The note is nothing of itself, but the actual tone it symbolizes does exist. In this same way, the symbol called money is nothing of itself. Yet the actual Supply does exist, which is symbolized by this appearance called money.

Everything that exists has a purpose in being. Thus, this aspect of Supply called money exists for a purpose. All activity that involves so-called money takes place as the fulfillment of a specific purpose.

This is true concerning that which we call investments, as in every transaction that involves money.

In our second volume of these classnotes, we will thoroughly explore the subject of Supply, Its purpose in being, and the way in which Its purpose is fulfilled. In this second volume, we are going to perceive clearly the way in which our perception that Spirit, Consciousness, is All—functions in and as every facet of our daily lives and experience. Once the subject of Supply is thoroughly understood, we shall have no so-called problems concerning Supply. For just now, suffice it to say that it is merely a false sense, a misinterpretation, of Supply, symbolized by an appearance that seems to present problems. Of course, the illusion of possession is the basic mistake.

All of the fancied problems vanish in the realization that *we are the Substance* of every investment. Furthermore, *we are the Activity* of every investment we are conscious of being. Indeed, we are the Substance, the Form, and the Activity of all that we see, hear, experience, or know. We are the activity of the Substance of every investment we have ever made or will ever make.

The activity of these investments cannot be in the nature of a loss because we cannot lose one iota of the Substance that we are. We know that the activity of every investment has to be right. It has to be intelligent activity because it is the Intelligence that we are, in action. And Intelligence makes no mistakes. Intelligence *always* fulfills Its purpose, and the purpose of these investments must be fulfilled. Having no problem of so-called ownership, we can simply depend upon the Mind that we are to function intelligently and perfectly in and *as* every aspect of our daily experience and affairs.

The illusion that we possess something, own something, is one of the aspects of nothingness that contributes to our false sense of limitation. We seem to burden ourselves with the "things" of the world, and then we let these "things" burden us. They seem to bind us. In fact, it even appears that they *possess us* and hold us in a viselike grip. It may appear that they form a circle around us, and this false sense of being encircled appears to interfere with our freedom. This same false sense makes it seem that we are separated from those called "others" and *our* possessions are separated in some way from the infinite, indivisible Supply which is Consciousness—the Consciousness that You are, that I am, and that Everyone is.

You know, it would seem that most of us struggle for years to attain "things." Then we may find it our fulfillment of purpose to relocate to some other section of our country, or even, perhaps, to reside in Europe, Africa, Asia, etc. Suddenly we feel burdened by all of these extraneous things we have supposedly acquired. Then a fallacious sense of limitation and of burden presents itself. We question, "How can I move and leave all of these treasures? If

I sold them, they would bring very little because they would have very little meaning to others. Yet if I have to move them, it entails much work and great expense." Thus we feel trapped and burdened by the very things we seem to have acquired. Again, we appear to be faced with the duality of limitation and a false sense of being burdened.

Now, of course, this does not mean that we should not be aware of an abundance of all Beauty, all comfort, convenience. On the contrary, we should be aware of unlimited abundance of Supply in every form and in every aspect in which Supply is evidenced. Neither does it mean that we should act unintelligently where Supply is concerned. It is all a matter of whether or not we permit Supply to bind or to burden us through a false sense of ownership.

Actually, students of the Ultimate should enjoy the best, the most beautiful things of the world. This is true because we know that the Consciousness we are is limitless, boundless, universal, and constant. We know there is no limitation of — or as — our Consciousness; thus, there is no limitation of the boundless abundance which comprises our Universe. You will again recall the statement in *Three Essential Steps*: "Your Consciousness is your Universe."

When we are free of the *false* sense of possession, we are really free to enjoy all the Beauty, the comforts, and all abundance which is normal in and as our experience. With no anxiety about these so-called "things," we are free to enjoy them to the fullest. We maintain our awareness that all of this Beauty and abundance exists within and *as* our Consciousness, and we know that we cannot possibly lose any of our Consciousness. We know the inexhaustible nature of our infinite Consciousness, and thus we know that the Supply that we *are* can never be depleted or exhausted. Knowing all of this Truth, we can thoroughly and freely enjoy all the Good, all the Beauty, all the Supply which we experience.

It is well to realize that there are many aspects of the illusion that we can possess something. For instance, there are some individuals who imagine that they "have" or "possess" good health. They go to great lengths in order to "obtain" this good health and to maintain it as their own possession. Back of all of this frenzy to keep their health, there is always a fear that they will lose it or be deprived of it in some way.

In fact, they seem to be so worried about losing this health that it becomes a burden to them. They seem to be afraid to eat or not to eat; afraid to exercise or not to exercise; they appear to be afraid to change climates or to go out in certain weather conditions. And there are some who seem to be dreadfully afraid of germs and any possible effect of contamination. In fact, these poor ones live in constant fear of being robbed of *their* health.

We do not mean that these deluded ones should be criticized. Always we must act from the standpoint of the Love that we are and know ourselves to be.

But we cannot avoid wishing that they could really be free to enjoy the health that they believe to be their possession. We can readily understand how it is that, believing that health is their possession, it would seem possible that they might be dispossessed of this health which they prize so highly.

Health does not *belong* to anyone. It is a Universal Existent, and It is eternally constant. Can you imagine what would happen to this Universe if It could be dispossessed of Its Health, Its Wholeness, Its Strength, etc.? God, this Universe, is Health Itself. We do not possess Health. Yet we are eternally and constantly in perfect health because we are perfect Health Itself. This leaves us completely free to thoroughly enjoy the Health that we are.

Of course, we do nothing foolish. We do not deliberately eat or drink anything that would be considered to have an adverse effect, any more than we would deliberately walk in front of a car. Nonetheless, we live perfectly normal, active lives without any seeming worry or anxiety about losing the Health we are and know ourselves to be.

We are all the Health, all the Wealth, all the complete Joy, Harmony, Peace, Perfection that is necessary to the complete fulfillment of the Universal Purpose; and of course, this means the fulfillment of our *specific* purpose in being. But this is not all. Within and *as* our Consciousness, there does constantly exist everything that is necessary to the complete, successful fulfillment of whatever may be our purpose at any given moment. *It is important that we be aware of the foregoing fact.*

You see, in the recognition of this vitally important fact, we discover our awareness of *why* we are. We realize why we exist. We find that we are aware of being all the strength, all the Intelligence, all the Consciousness of whatever is necessary for our fulfillment of purpose. We find that we *are* the health, the harmony, the control, the stability, even the constancy that is necessary for our fulfillment of purpose.

There is another aspect of very great importance in the realization of being all that is necessary to our fulfillment of purpose. We must know that *we are Mind.* We must realize that we are the omnipresent, omniactive, omnipotent Intelligence that knows what every purpose is and knows how to be the fulfillment of every purpose. In this "knowing," there can be no mistakes; there can be no failures. There can be no unintelligent decisions or acts.

In our booklet, *Success Is Normal*, we have explored this aspect of our Being quite thoroughly. Therefore, we will not elaborate on this subject just now. However, the subject is infinite and has innumerable ramifications. In the second volume of these classnotes, we will pursue at much greater length just how it is, and why it is, impossible to make mistakes or to fail when we are aware of *being* limitless, boundless Mind, fulfilling Its purpose in being *our* fulfillment of purpose.

Sometimes we falsely imagine that we can possess Love. It is as though the love of someone belonged to us. This fallacy always leads to a false sense of fear or uncertainty. If it seems that we possess the love of someone, it is also going to appear that we can be dispossessed of this love.

Many ugly pictures can rear their illusory heads in such a seeming situation. Among these phantasmic pictures may be jealousy, which really is nothing other than illusory hatred. Another of these delusions is fear. We may fear that "something will happen" to one we call our child, our husband, or some loved one. Thus, we appear to be afraid that we will lose these dear ones. All of us have known those who were apparently so fearful of losing a loved one that they could not fully enjoy his or her presence in daily living. Fear is indeed a dreadful illusion.

When we perceive the indivisible Nature of all conscious, living, intelligent Love, we *know* that we cannot possibly "lose" anyone. The Consciousness that we are is inseparable from the Consciousness of our loved ones. We can no more lose a loved one than we can lose our own Consciousness. Let us realize this Truth and be free to thoroughly enjoy our dear ones right here and now.

We can never be free so long as it seems to us that we possess anyone. There is no freedom in the illusion of possession. We can never possess anyone. No one can ever possess us. This being true, we can never lose anyone, and no one can lose us. The only genuine Love in existence is that Love which leaves everyone completely free and that is completely free Itself from any false sense of ownership.

Do you know that we do not really possess anything? We do not even possess a life of our own or a consciousness of our own. Yes, we can go further than that and realize that we do not possess a body of our own. God *is* All; All *is* God. The Life we have called our own really belongs to God. It is God living. It is God alive. If there were no God, there would be no Life to be alive. How, then, can we claim to possess a Life of our own? We can't!

All anxiety for Life is obliterated when we realize that God really is the *only* Life; furthermore, that God really is the only Life that is *ever* alive. This means freedom from all fear or concern about Life. Oh, it is so wonderful to realize that we need not be fearful or concerned about the eternal Life that is alive as the Life of everyone and everything. Wonderful things take place when we are completely free from fear or anxiety for our loved ones or for ourselves. It will be well to contemplate this section of this book pertaining to Life.

All that is true as Life is also true as Consciousness. Sometimes it *appears* that a loss of Consciousness is threatened or has taken place. No one can lose Consciousness because no one possesses Consciousness. It is God who is Consciousness. It is God who is the *only* Consciousness. God is the very conscious Life that is alive as this Consciousness, this Life, right here and now. One can no more lose Consciousness than he can lose himself because living Consciousness is the Self of each one of us.

It would be well to consider at least one more aspect of the illusory sense of possession. This aspect is Body. It may seem to us that surely we possess our own Body. But do we? Let us consider this Body for a few moments, and we will discover how impossible it is for us to own the Body.

What is the Essence of the Body? There is no matter, as such, so it cannot be matter. Even the greatest of the physicists know that matter, as it appears to be, is nothing but illusion. Nonetheless, we know that there is Substance right here as this Body.

What is Substance? God really is all Substance. But perhaps that is putting it a bit too simply. So let us really know what God is as the Substance of this Body. Consciousness is the only Substance in existence. That which we call Spirit is really Consciousness. But Consciousness is inseparable from Life, Mind, and Love. There is no way to separate these indivisible aspects of Existence. This being true, the Body has to consist of Life, Consciousness, Mind, Love. Therefore, the Substance in Form that is this Body consists of eternal, living, intelligent, loving Consciousness.

We have seen that it is impossible for us to possess Life, Mind, Love, Consciousness. Now it is equally clear that it is impossible for us to possess a Body that consists of this indivisible Essence or Substance.

# Chapter XII

# Universal and Specific
# Purpose Fulfilled

Sometimes it seems that all the so-called "powers that be" are in league against us. It appears that there is something always trying to stop us or to interfere with the fulfillment of our purpose in being. Perhaps our environment seems all wrong. There may appear to be situations in our office, our home, or in our professional experience that tend to irk us, block us, or otherwise deter us.

Of course, this is all illusory. Nonetheless, it can seem very real indeed. And these seeming factors can certainly appear to frustrate, defy, or to defeat our very best so-called human efforts. Please be assured that this same illusion that seems to plague those of us who are in the business or professional world also appears to frustrate those of us who are homemakers.

Despite any appearance of frustrating influences, etc., there is the right Truth, or the right "way" — if you prefer that terminology — to perceive that which is true and to experience the evidence of the Truth we perceive. Let us now see what must be realized in any situation in which it seems difficult to *be* the fulfillment of our purpose in being.

First of all, let us discover *why* we are engaged in any specific activity. Are we performing this activity merely for the purpose of "making" more money? Is our activity only for our own little so-called personal need or gratification? How unselfed is our activity?

Beloved, the bigness, the greatness, of our fulfillment will certainly depend, to a great extent, upon our conscious bigness, our conscious greatness. And this limitless bigness does manifest Itself as the fulfillment of a great purpose. Please be assured that our fulfillment of purpose is always as great, as limitless, as we are and know ourselves to be.

If it seems to us that we are little, limited, self-seeking persons, then our fulfillment of purpose will also seem to be small, unsatisfying, and even frustrating. So, the first requisite in our activity is to be fully aware of our universal, indivisible, boundless, limitless Nature. As we are increasingly aware of *being what we are*, we find our business or professional activity or our activity in the home is increasingly unlimited and so satisfying.

If our fulfillment of purpose seems to be limited, it is only because we appear to limit this fulfillment of purpose. If we falsely imagine that we have a separate purpose of our own to fulfill, we have, in that very delusion, limited our fulfillment of purpose. Complete, joyous, satisfying fulfillment of purpose can only be realized when we recognize the inseparable Nature of all Existence and of all fulfillment of Purpose. It is always the illusory little "I" that deludes itself into imaginary self-importance, self-satisfaction, self-sufficiency. It is in this way that it appears to separate itself from the Infinite All; thus, it also seems to limit itself in all ways. We must "see" further than this little illusory "I." In other words, we must perceive the universal, indivisible Nature of all Truth, all living, conscious, loving Mind. Only in this way can we realize the limitless fulfillment of Purpose, which is both Universal and specific.

In our consideration of being the fulfillment of any purpose, it is necessary first to contemplate from the Universal standpoint. It is in this way that we contemplate in and *as* the absolute, complete, inseparable Entirety of all Being. Then we can be sure that our contemplation is free from all duality. We can know that our contemplation is completely impersonal and that we are not contemplating from any little limited, selfish standpoint.

Oh, there is great power in this universal, loving, unselfed contemplation. In fact, there is Universal Omnipotence in action, as our Consciousness, in this wholly unselfish contemplation. The seeming limitations, frustrations, and struggles literally melt into oblivion when we contemplate in and *as* the Entirety which is the Universe Itself. There is no little "I" in this limitless, unselfed way of contemplation.

In this impersonal way of "seeing," we can be sure that no selfishness enters into our contemplation.

Here, we are in the "Holy of Holies." We are completely free from any so-called human desires, ambitions, or hopes. In this way, we are free from all struggle, strain, or strife.

# Chapter XIII

## Purposeful Contemplation

We have said that everyone and everything exists for the fulfillment of a universal, as well as a specific, purpose. We have also stated that all activity takes place for the fulfillment of a universal and specific purpose. Contemplation is an activity of conscious Mind, or intelligent Consciousness. This glorious activity is the fulfillment of a universal, as well as a specific, purpose. Hence, all contemplation is purposeful contemplation.

Often someone will inquire as to the "method" of contemplation. It appears that some clarification is necessary pertaining to this important aspect of our activity. No method for contemplation can be given because each one of us is his own revelator and his own revelation. However, a few guideposts may be presented, and in this way, some of the seeming pitfalls may be avoided. Furthermore, our contemplation will be clear and purposeful.

First of all, it is necessary to understand the distinction between meditation and contemplation. It seems there has been much confusion about these two words. Although they are sometimes used interchangeably, there is a definite distinction in the meaning of these two words. In order to clarify this distinction, let us consult Webster's Dictionary. Here, the definition of *meditation* includes the following:

Act of meditation; close or continued thought.

The word *contemplation* is defined as:

Act of the mind in considering with attention; act of viewing steadfastly and attentively.

We can see that a definite distinction exists between these two definitions. It is well to consider this distinction between the words *meditation* and *contemplation*.

In order to further clarify this subject, we will first consider the word *meditation*. You see, the "act of continued thought" is one of the pitfalls we mentioned a moment ago. *Infinite Mind does not think; It knows constantly and eternally.* Any effort to think has to do with the little assumptive mind of illusory "man with breath in his nostrils." And any so-called activity of this assumptive mind is, of necessity, labored and faulty.

Meditation begins by focusing the attention and concentration of the so-called mind of illusory man at a given point. There is always an effort to literally "pull" the attention to this point or this subject. Therefore, the first activity of meditation involves effort. But this is not all. This very attempt to concentrate at a given point means to concentrate on limitation. Starting from a limited premise, the perception must be limited. It is only the fallacious mind of assumptive man that limits itself in this way or that strives to concentrate. At best, this kind of meditation can only perceive from the standpoint of its own limitations. At worst, it can certainly seem to be self-hypnotic. And this self-hypnosis should be avoided as perhaps the worst pitfall of all.

Now let us examine the word *contemplation* and see why contemplation is natural and right for students of the Ultimate. There is no mental effort in contemplation. If we seem to strive to contemplate, we are not contemplating at all.

To contemplate is to consider, to view, Existence as It is. For example, we may hear a beautiful symphony and attentively consider this Beauty. If we are educated in music, we may even consider the various aspects of Beauty that contribute to its complete perfection. The Beauty of the music *is*.

Then, too, we may look into the heart of a rose. We may consider the wonderful perfection of the petal formation, the glorious Beauty of its coloring, or the fine vein-like lines so perfectly displayed. In either case, we make no effort in our viewing, our consideration, of the complete Beauty of the music or the rose. Yet our attention is, at the moment, focused upon the specific Beauty of either the music or the rose.

Then, too, we may look up and consider the beautiful ever-active cloud patterns or the wonderful, indescribable blue of a summer sky. At night, we may literally lose ourselves in viewing the stars, the moon, the clouds, etc. Oh, there is much Truth that may be revealed through the effortless consideration of the wondrous night skies. But these limitless revelations could not be experienced if we were to try to analyze these spaceless skies. Neither could they take place if we were to make any effort to "think out" the answers that seem to be hidden in these open skies.

Our contemplation is purposeful. Yet this purpose is not fulfilled by concentrated thought. It is completely effortless. Certainly it is free from limitations of any kind. Can we imagine the infinite Universal Mind that is God having to think or to reason in order to know that which does exist? Of course not. And what Mind could we be other than the Mind that is God?

Never do we begin our contemplation from a limited standpoint. Never do we try to pull our attention into a little limited point or subject and then attempt to think our way out from that limited point. Rather, our contemplation begins from the standpoint of the limitless, boundless Universe Itself, which is God. Beginning with an unlimited premise, our revelations are without limits or boundaries. By this same token, we do not begin our contemplation from the standpoint of the specific. Rather, we begin this wonderful activity from the standpoint of the boundless, infinite All.

Now, before we begin our actual contemplative exploration, there are questions which are necessary to answer. The following are typical of the numerous questions that have been asked by students of the Ultimate. For instance, "When should I contemplate? How long should I remain in contemplation? Should I assume any particular posture while contemplating? How will I know when my period of contemplation should end? How do I approach this contemplation from the Universal standpoint?"

No one can tell you when to contemplate. I have found it to be exceedingly wonderful to contemplate shortly after I have rested—slept. (Actually, what we call sleep is simply active rest.) However, it is possible to reach a point where we are already in contemplation when we awaken. But this takes place when we constantly walk *in* the Light *as* the Light. However, most students find it very helpful to contemplate as much as possible during the morning, then to return to their contemplation as often as possible during the afternoon and evening. Some of us awaken often during the night and contemplate when we awaken.

Contemplation absorbs our full attention. Thus, it is well to be free from any so-called pressing duties immediately following this activity. If, during our quiet period, we have any concern for some important so-called human activity that we just have to engage in immediately after our contemplation, there is a tendency to try to "see" as much as we can during our silence. This, of course, is diverting, and it also results in a false sense of effort. This is why it is well to contemplate just before retiring for the night and to be in contemplation as we go to sleep. Ofttimes the Consciousness goes right on with whatever It is perceiving throughout the night. (We never lose Consciousness, and Consciousness never becomes inactive.)

Your period of contemplation may be culminated in just a few moments. It may be an hour, or several hours, before you know that this period of contemplation is finished. If you simply must go about your daily affairs before you feel this Absolute Completeness, you can always return to this activity later in the day or night. Furthermore, you will find that you have lost nothing of the continuity of your "seeing." You just know that you are the same Consciousness that you were when you were in contemplation.

In any event, you will know when your contemplation is sufficient for the moment. It is as though an unseen Presence says, "It is finished." You sense it. You actually "feel" this assurance flowing and surging through and *as* your entire Body. When this takes place you can freely and joyously begin whatever activity is necessary. If you try to remain in contemplation after you have sensed the "signal" that it is finished, you will begin to feel restless or the necessity for other activity will announce itself. In the *Gospel According to Thomas*, we read, "There is a movement, and there is a rest." This is true; and it has great significance.

Assume any posture that is comfortable for you when in contemplation. Any unnatural or uncomfortable position will invariably seem to make you aware of the body. Just be comfortable.

Now, for the last and most important question: you approach this contemplation from the Universal standpoint by becoming completely unaware of the fictitious little "I" and by actually being "full open" Consciousness.

Of course, no one can use a method or a formula for this preparation. To do this would mean to "think" or to go through certain "thought processes." In this way, you would become involved in an effort, and this would defeat the whole purpose of your contemplation. Nonetheless, it is necessary that the little assumptive "I" be transcended.

I have often found it to be most helpful when some statement of Truth pertaining to the Allness of God appears within and *as* the Consciousness I am. For instance, sometimes I will find myself saying:

> God *is* All; *All* is *God*. Just imagine, what could "I" be if God were not All? If God were not All, there could be no me.

Oh, the statements come. I don't try to think them or anything like that. But always the first few statements are those that reveal the Allness that is God and the nothingness of any little assumptive "I" named "Marie."

You will find that the statements are always fresh and new, and this is as it should be. But whatever the statements may be, just rest in them until you actually "feel" the Allness that is God, *being* the Allness that is You. It is as though a loving, liquid warmth flowed throughout your entire Being. Generally, there is no sense of Body at all. It is just God being all there is of you.

Beloved, you will find the way that is right for you. You will discover the way in which the assumptive little "I" most quickly dissolves.

For many students of the Ultimate and for myself, the way is revealed as we "consider the heavens, the work of his hands." Consider the limitless, boundless vastness that is this Universe. *This is God!* Consider the wonder that It does not begin, nor can It end. Consider the Truth that It has neither center nor circumference.

Consider the countless galaxies that are so constantly, intelligently active. Consider the uncountable stars and planets that so-called man has never discovered. Consider the wonderful, omnipotent, living Intelligence that is God, *being* this Universe — yes, God being every star, every planet, every sun and moon. And God really *is* Spirit. This Universe consists of God, Spirit. Every star, every planet, sun, and moon is the Presence of God and of nothing else. No little self now. Just God, God, *God!*

Now you are ready. Now you are "full open." And it is in this "full openness" that the omnipotent,

Almighty God—the All—fulfills Its purpose infinitely and specifically.

We have said that all contemplation was—and is—purposeful. But we must be very alert here. Never do we have any specific purpose to be accomplished during our contemplation. We simply contemplate the Allness *as* the Allness Itself, knowing full well that our contemplation is Its own fulfillment of Its own purpose.

It is true, we do contemplate various aspects of the Infinite All. For instance, we may find ourselves in a contemplation in which Universal Life is of paramount importance. Again, our contemplation may be literally surging with the revelations of infinite, eternal, immutable Consciousness.

Mind, Intelligence, may be the outstanding aspect of a contemplation period; or perhaps it may be Love. Ah! The contemplation which is Love in action is the most glorious of all. And we find that no matter what aspect of God is revealed most powerfully, *Love is always the basic or underlying power of the contemplation.*

Now we have mentioned Life, Consciousness, Mind, Love. These four aspects of God—the Universal All—are indivisibly One. Life is Consciousness, Mind, Love. Consciousness is Life, Mind, Love. Mind is Life, Consciousness, Love. Love is Life, Consciousness, Mind. These four basic aspects of the One inseparable All are always present within and as the Consciousness of everyone and everything.

However, when our attention is absorbed in contemplation, we are intensely aware of their presence. Although one of these aspects of God may claim more of our attention than another during a contemplative period, yet there is always an awareness of the fact that God is completely omnipresent—forever, equally, and eternally.

Now, it is regrettable that we must divert our attention for a moment. This is necessary in order that we perceive how—in what way—the purpose of our contemplation is fulfilled. Some of what is to follow will sound dualistic, but students of the Ultimate will understand the Absolute Oneness of all existence, regardless of the "words" that are necessary to convey the meaning.

The illusion called fear seems to underlie every so-called problem. This fictitious imposition may manifest itself in many ways. But the basic illusions of fear have to do with Life, Mind, Consciousness, Love. Not that these illusions ever touch this inseparable Allness; but rather, there appears to be a great ignorance, or unawareness, of the Completeness—the eternal, perfect All—which is ever present.

The illusory fear that seems to be most prevalent is the fear of death. Yet death is considered inevitable. It is paradoxical that the greatest illusion, called fear of death, should be based in something that is believed inevitable. To fear death means to fear loss of Life, loss of Consciousness, loss of Intelligence, loss of Love, loss of Identity, loss of Body.

As you can see, these illusory fears are all involved with so-called loss. Therefore, the constant, eternal Omnipresence of eternal, uninterrupted Life, Mind, Consciousness, will always be of the greatest importance in every period of contemplation. Purposeful contemplation reveals the forever Truth that eternal, constant Life, and the conscious Mind that is aware of being eternal Life, comprise the only Consciousness, the only Mind, in Existence. This wonderful revelation precludes the possibility of a mind that can fear. Actually, fear is unknown because it is unknown to the One and *Only* conscious, living, loving Mind, God.

As you contemplate in this way, you will find the word *Love* becoming increasingly important. You will perceive that omnipotent, living, conscious Love is completely fearless. Knowing nothing other than Itself, it can know nothing to fear. Now you can see that Life, Consciousness, Mind, Love are all present within and as your contemplation when some illusion called fear seems to be brought to your attention.

There are many aspects of the illusion called fear. For instance, fear of pain, fear of failure, fear of accident, fear of inadequacy, etc. However, it makes no difference what aspect of this illusion may seem to present itself, the contemplative awareness of the omnipresent, omnipotent, indivisible, living, conscious, intelligent Love that is All fulfills Its purpose; then this horrendous illusion is dispelled.

Contemplation from the Universal standpoint always reveals the nothingness of whatever seems to be a problem. For instance, if it appears that someone is threatened by death, our contemplation will reveal the boundless Presence of Universal Life.

But—make no mistake about this—we do not do anything mentally in the nature of a declaration or a so-called treatment. Rather, it is that because a seeming problem called "fear of death" has presented itself, our Universal Consciousness of eternal, constant, omnipresent, omnipotent Life reveals Itself to be uppermost in our contemplation.

*We do nothing of ourselves.* We do not try to take a so-called problem into our contemplation. Rather, we simply are aware of being full open Consciousness, and whatever the Truth *is*—instead of what the illusion *seems* to be—immediately reveals Itself powerfully and clearly. This is why, if death seems imminent or there is a fear of death, our awareness of Universal Life, in all of Its completeness and eternality, will be evident without any effort at all.

In a situation such as the foregoing, we will discover that as "full open" Consciousness, we are considering the boundless Universe. Life is activity; thus, we may contemplate the innumerable galaxies in their perfect orbiting. We may contemplate the countless billions of stars and planets—most of them still undiscovered by so-called man. No doubt our contemplation will reveal the fact that eternal Life exists universally and that It exists in, on, and *as* every star, every planet, etc. Our contemplation will reveal that even though all Life is manifested in Form, still all is universal, eternal, and indivisible. We will perceive that Life is all that is ever alive. We will also perceive that Life lives Itself and that Life is responsible for Its own maintenance and eternality. In short, all concern for a so-called human, temporary life is completely dispelled.

Beloved, do you see what has taken place in this contemplation? We have transcended all seeming personal sense, all illusion concerning a personal life or body. We have perceived Life as God perceives Life. And this perception has been God aware of being the *only* Life that is ever alive.

You will find that virtually every period of contemplation fulfills its purpose in much the same way. There will be an ever-increasing awareness of the indivisibility of universal, impersonal Life, Mind, Consciousness, Love. There will be an ever greater and more powerful awareness that *there is One Life, One Mind, One Consciousness, One Love* and that this conscious, living, intelligent Love is never divided into separate minds, lives, consciousnesses, loves.

Herein is the infinite Power of our "seeing." It really takes the Mind that is God to contemplate in this way. It is the Consciousness that is aware of *being* the omnipotent Omnipresence that is the only Life, the only One who is alive; the only Mind, the only One who is intelligent; the only Consciousness, the only One who is conscious; the only Love, the only One who loves. And basically, this is what is revealed during every period of contemplation.

Suppose a so-called problem should be presented which has to do with Mind. You do not dwell on the fictitious problem. Why dwell on nothing? Furthermore, there would be no fulfillment of purpose in being trapped with the illusion. Never can you see beyond the illusion so long as you dawdle along with it. Let the illusion delude itself. It will all be dispelled in your contemplation of the presence of the "Somethingness" rather than the "nothingness" that claims to be present.

When an illusion of imperfect mind appears, your contemplation will reveal intense activity and perception as that aspect of the Allness which is Mind, or Intelligence. Again you will be "full open." You will perceive the Universal Nature of all-living, conscious, loving Mind. You will perceive that this Universe is an intelligent Universe. Your contemplation will reveal the infinite Intelligence in action, which governs and controls Itself as this Universe. The absolute, perfect, orderly activity of the galaxies, the stars, the planets, the suns and moons will be apparent in this contemplation. You will be aware of the supreme Intelligence in action, which governs so perfectly the orbiting of our Earth Planet. Perhaps the marvel of the precise movement of the tides will intrigue you.

Mind, as an infinite variety of Its own manifestations, will reveal Itself as you contemplate. All the while, Intelligence is uppermost in your contemplation, but you will continue to be aware of Life, Love, and Consciousness. You will—without effort —realize the inseparability of Mind from living, conscious Love. You will know that conscious, living, loving Mind is alive. It is conscious. It is loving. It is Life because It is alive. And It is all of this, being supremely intelligent, because It is Mind being Itself.

In this glorious contemplation, you will perceive that conscious, living, loving Mind—Intelligence—is unconfined and uncontained. It is unconditioned. You will know the meaning of Jesus' statement as reported in *The Gospel According to Thomas* "Cleave a piece of wood; I am there. Lift up the stone, and you will find me there."

Oh yes, you will certainly perceive that the universal, living, loving, conscious Mind that You are is everywhere because *this Mind is the Everywhere.*

You will *know* that the boundless Mind you are is the unconfined Intelligence that is intelligent equally everywhere and eternally. You will perceive that this boundless, constant Mind that you are is the one and only Intelligence that is identified as Everyone—here, now, infinitely and eternally.

In the foregoing quotation, Jesus was being both Universal and specific in his statement. He was actually saying that the universal, living, loving, conscious Mind was indivisibly present as the Universe and as the piece of wood or the stone.

Beloved, it is this glorious perception of the Universal—as well as the specific—Mind that reveals the Presence of perfect Intelligence right where a so-called troubled mind has seemed to be.

If, while in this contemplation, anyone were to tell you that Intelligence was centered in a so-called brain and confined to a temporary body, you would marvel at such gross ignorance. You would be so aware of the *fact* of the Omnipresence which is Mind that any statement of what Mind is *not* would be ridiculous. Your very awareness of the universal, indivisible, constant nature of Mind would be your immunity to any illusions concerning this boundless Intelligence.

We have spoken of our contemplation in which the foremost aspects of the universal, inseparable One are Life and Mind, or living Mind. We may also refer to this living Mind as Intelligent Life.

Now let us consider our contemplation when its most perceptible aspect is Consciousness. Consciousness is Spirit. Spirit is the Substance, the Essence, of all Form. (This does not mean that Consciousness is separated from Life, Love, Mind.) Nonetheless, the words *Consciousness, Spirit, Substance, Essence* are interchangeable, for their meaning is identical. When, in contemplation, Consciousness—Awareness —becomes uppermost as our awareness, we know that some illusory problem concerning Substance— the Body—is being transcended.

We do not deliberately try to compel Consciousness to be uppermost in our contemplation. However, it is uppermost because an illusory misconception of some Substance of the Body has or is presenting itself. Suppose, for instance, that it appears that some aspect of the Body is deteriorating. Suppose that it seems to have become infected, infested, incomplete, or in some way impaired or imperfect. During our contemplation, Consciousness is revealed to be the *only* Substance, rather than the phantasmal pictures which have presented themselves.

We have heard and read much about the spiritual Body. We know that many individuals have seen and experienced *being* the Body of Light. This has become such a frequent experience with so many Identities that it can no longer be ridiculed or denied. Indeed, there is a Body that consists of Spirit, or Light. Furthermore, this Body of Light is the *only* Body. There are not two bodies, one a Body of Light and the other a body of darkness, solidity, density.

Consciousness is the Substance of the only Body. Consciousness is the eternal, immutable, birthless, ageless, deathless Essence that is manifested in Form as the Body of Spirit, Light. However, the Body is alive. It is intelligent, and It is perfect and harmonious. Life alone is alive; Mind alone is intelligent; Love alone is loving; and Consciousness alone is conscious. Therefore, you can perceive that the Essence—Consciousness—that comprises the Body is also Life, Mind, and Love. And there is no way in which this inseparable Oneness can be divided into bits and parts of Itself. Nonetheless, when a specific purpose is to be fulfilled, your contemplation will be literally flooded with the aspect of Consciousness which is Body.

Consciousness—Awareness of Being—*is* this boundless Universe. Every one and every thing in Existence is Consciousness, aware of *being* what It *is*. All Substance is Consciousness, aware of being. All Substance in Form is Consciousness, aware of being. Consciousness can only be aware of Itself—of what It *is*—because there is nothing other than Consciousness for Consciousness to be aware of or to know.

Consciousness is eternal, uninterrupted Perfection. Thus, all Substance is Consciousness, aware of being eternal, uninterrupted Perfection. All Substance in Form is Consciousness aware of being eternal, uninterrupted Perfection. The Substance in Form that comprises your Body, as well as the Body of everyone and everything, is Consciousness in Form, aware of being eternal, uninterrupted Perfection. This, beloved, is your Body of Light, or Spirit, *and you are this body of light.*

Let your contemplation reveal how it is, and why it is, that you *are* this Body of Light. You will realize that you are conscious, and there is nothing that can be conscious other than Consciousness. The Consciousness that you are is your very awareness that you exist. Thus, your awareness that you exist is the Consciousness that you are, aware of being the perfect, eternal Substance in Form that is your eternal Body.

Contemplation will reveal the foregoing to be an Absolute Truth or Fact. But more than this, contemplation will reveal that this Universal Absolute Fact exists specifically as the Identity that you are and *as the eternal Body that you are.*

You exist as the fulfillment of a Universal purpose. You exist as a specific Identity and as a specific Body, in order that this purpose may be completely fulfilled. If you did not exist as *you*, the Universal purpose could not be completely fulfilled. If the Body you are did not exist *as this Body*, your specific, as well as your Universal, purpose could not be fulfilled.

The fact that you exist as a specific Identity does not mean that you are separated in any way from the Universal Oneness that you are. The fact that you are a specific Body does not mean that this Body is separate from the Universal Oneness that is the boundless Body of God. It is only because you are universal, living, intelligent, loving Consciousness that you can be a specific Identity. It is only because you are universal, living, loving, conscious Mind that you can be—and know your Self to be—this specific Body. In other words, the Body is both Universal and specific, and It is absolutely necessary to both the Universal and the specific fulfillment of purpose.

In order to constantly fulfill Its purpose, the Body has to be perfect, and It has to remain constantly and eternally perfect. It is perfect because It consists of the Universal Awareness of being the Perfection that *you are*. It remains constantly and eternally perfect because It consists of the eternal, constant, uninterrupted Consciousness of Being that *you are*, aware of being eternal, constant, uninterrupted Perfection.

Beloved, we can say no more pertaining to the Body in this first volume of our classnotes. However, in our second volume, we will go all the way in the revelation of *what* the Body is, and *why* the Body is what the Body is. What has been given here is a thorough preparation for the further revelation of the eternal, perfect Body. I sincerely hope that you will conscientiously read, study —and above all— contemplate the Truths revealed in this first volume before you read the second volume of this revelation. The book to follow will be much more specific, and it will thoroughly reveal the way in which this Absolute Ultimate Truth fulfills Its purpose in and *as* every aspect of your daily affairs, your home, your business or profession, and your Body.

We have now realized the omnipotent Omnipresence of Life, Mind, and Consciousness. We have intentionally left the most important aspect of our Existence to be revealed as the finale of this volume. We must now fully perceive the dynamic, vital Principle of this entire revelation, and this irresistible Principle is Love. Without Love, all our contemplation would be "as sounding brass, or a tinkling cymbal" (1 Cor. 13:1). Without Love, our contemplation would be futile indeed. No purpose could be fulfilled if Love were not always present within and *as* our entire Being.

It is true that either Life or Mind may be the outstanding aspect of our contemplation; and many times Consciousness is uppermost as we contemplate. But Love must forever and constantly be the omniactive Presence, the motivating Power, of all contemplation. No matter what aspect of our Entirety may be foremost in any specific contemplation, Love is the basic, the primary Essence of our Existence. And Love must always be perceived, experienced, yes, even felt, throughout every period of contemplation. Furthermore, this glorious All, Love, must be the basic Principle that guides, governs, and controls every aspect of our daily lives and experiences.

Love is the Fire of this whole revelation. Love is the Inspiration. Love is the warmth, the joy, the peace; the surging, glowing, omniactive Essence that is our entire Being. Love is Perfection. Love is all Truth. Love is Life; Love is Mind; Love is Consciousness. Love is God. And *you* have no choice other than to be just what God — Love — is.

Oh, if there were but one word in the English language, let this word be *Love*. Love is the perfect and complete answer to every seeming sorrow, pain, trouble, fear, or whatever appears to plague us. So, beloved one, let us really perceive and understand the Love that is God and the God that is Love.

In order to perceive what Love is, we must first understand what Love is not. Perhaps there is less understanding of the word *Love* than there is a clear perception of any word in our language. In the phantasmic world of sheer illusion, terrible things seem to parade under the guise of Love. All of us have apparently been brought face to face with the subtle, deceptive nature of that nothingness that pretends to be personal love.

Let us not dwell long with this travesty. Suffice it to say that all seeming injustice, all the supposed human suffering that appears to be inflicted by the fantasy called personal love is obliterated when we really know what Love *is* and when we know that *we are Universal Love.*

Love, in order to be Love, has to be perfect, complete, entire. Perfect Love is absolute. Therefore, Love is entire, whole, pure. It must also be unlimited, unrestricted, and unqualified. Love is limitless and boundless. Love is an eternal Universal Constant. Love is as indivisible as is Universal Consciousness, Life, Mind, because Love *is* universal, living, conscious Mind.

Love is a living, omnipresent Essence. It is omnipotent because It is Omnipotence. It exists everywhere and eternally because It is the Everywhere, and It is the Eternality of all Existence. Love is an active Essence. It is omniactive, conscious Mind. It is free from all illusory misconceptions. It is the Power of every contemplation. It is the Presence that is ever gentle, although It is ever firm. It is irresistible in and as Its flowing, surging, omnipotent, omnipresent, universal Allness. Oh, how can Love, the glorious, wordless word, be stated here in mere words? It really can't. Yet the words come, and they must be presented.

It is Love that is our inseparable Oneness. It is Love that makes our entire Existence perfect, joyous, and peaceful. It is Love that fulfills Its purpose *as* our Perfection, as our perfect, harmonious activity and as our Entirety. It is Love that precludes the possibility of fear, dread, or sorrow. It is Love that is the Light that we are.

It is Love that acts so perfectly as the Universal Oneness, the Universal All, in action. It is Love that acts so perfectly as each specific "I." It is Love that makes the Universal and the specific inseparably One. It is Love, the Universal *I*, being the specific "I." It is Love that is evident as the perfect, harmonious activity of each and every galaxy, every star and planet, every sun and moon. It is Love that is evidenced as their perfect, harmonious activity as specific—yet indivisible, Universal—aspects of the Entirety, the Totality, God.

Love does not divide Itself into loves. Love has no object. It is equally present and equally Love everywhere and eternally. It does not come. It does not go. There is no vacuum in Love. There is no interim, no interval, and no interruption in Love. Love is a steady, constant, integral, omnipotent, omniactive Presence. Love is a Wholeness, an indivisible Entirety, a Totality. Love is complete within and *as* Itself. It asks for nothing. It needs nothing. It is conscious Allness, conscious Perfection, conscious Freedom, Bliss, Ecstasy. Love is always illumined, for Love is illumined Consciousness.

Love is never *in* love. Love *is* Love! Love has no choice but to love because It has no choice to be other than the Love that It eternally and universally is. Love is always unselfed. It is compassionate. Yet It acts intelligently, even though It is understanding and compassionate. It does not condone any false appearance of the nothingness called evil. It is never deceived. It is never imposed upon; It never imposes.

Being Intelligence, It always sees right through any so-called mask of deception. Yet It does not condemn. Neither does It become resentful. Being Love, It cannot hate or even dislike. It is Its own immunity to every so-called attempt to defeat or to destroy. It is completely impervious to any and all shafts of illusory evil. It just goes right on being the intelligent Love that It is and knows Itself to be.

Love's kingdom is not of this world. Therefore, It is not subject to the so-called illusions and delusions of a world made of fantasies. It "walks around in the dream, awake." It knows what the dream and the dreamer seem to be and to experience. Yet Love perceives the Reality, the Eternal, to be all there is of the one who seems to be dreaming and thus perceives the nothingness of any dream.

Love is the Perfection of all Beauty. Love is the Beauty of all Perfection. Love is the one, universal, intelligent, conscious, living Essence. Love is the Perfection that is the Substance of all Form, the Form of all Substance. Love is the omnipotent Omniaction that acts so perfectly as the activity of all Substance in Form, and the Form of all Substance. It is Love that fulfills Its eternal, Universal purpose by being eternally, universally present and purposefully active.

It is Love that is evident as the Beauty of the rose, the glory of the setting sun, or the song of the bird. It is Love that is evident as the blue of the sky, the green of the grass, the iridescence of the leaves dancing so gracefully in the sunlight. It is Love that is evident as the silent, spaceless Beauty of the desert, the grandeur of the mountains, the soft, gentle whispering of the stream, and the joyous play of the sun on the fountain. It is Love that is evident as the Beauty of all Substance in Form. It is Love that is evident as the Beauty of the Form of all Substance.

It is Love that is evident as the Perfection of the Beauty that *you are*. It is Love that is evident as the Beauty of Perfection which comprises your Substance and the Form of your Substance.

Love is evidenced as the perfect harmony and Beauty of your home and your environment. Love is evidenced as the perfect, harmonious activity of your daily affairs. Love is evidenced as the perfect, harmonious activity of your business, your profession, or that which is called your labor. Love is evidenced as the perfect, harmonious, unlabored, effortless movement of every event of your day and night. All is Love; Love is All.

Now, where and what is this Allness that is universal, eternal Love? Beloved, It is always where you are because It is what you are. This is why you can never be separated from Love's omnipresent Harmony, Beauty, Wholeness, Completeness. You can never be separated from your Self because you are alive as your Self. Because you are intelligent, you are Mind. Because you are conscious, you are Consciousness. Because you are alive, you are Life. Because you are loving, you are Love.

You are the evidence of the fact that living, intelligent, conscious Love *is*. You are the evidence of the fact that intelligent, conscious, living Mind *is*. You are the evidence of the fact that loving, living, Consciousness *is*. You are the evidence of the fact that conscious, loving, intelligent Life *is*. All of this you are, beloved, because *this is all you are.* Thus it is. Thus it remains eternally.

> Know your Self. Be your Self. For the Love you are is the *only* Self you are.

# About the Author

During early childhood, Marie S. Watts began questioning: "Why am I? What am I? Where is God? What is God?"

After experiencing her first illumination at seven years of age, her hunger for the answers to these questions became intensified. Although she became a concert pianist, her search for the answers continued, leading her to study all religions, including those of the East.

Finally, ill and unsatisfied, she gave up her profession of music, discarded all books of ancient and modern religions, kept only the Bible, and went into virtual seclusion from the world for some eight years. It was out of the revelations and illuminations she experienced during those years, revelations that were sometimes the very opposite of what she had hitherto believed, that her own healing was realized and that her book *The Ultimate* came.

During all the previous years, she had been active in helping others. After *The Ultimate* was published, she devoted herself exclusively to the continuance of the healing work and to lecturing and teaching.

Revelations continued to come to her from within her own consciousness, and they were set forth as she did in this book.

To all seekers for Light, for Truth, for God, for an understanding of their own true Being, this book will serve as a revolutionary but wholly satisfying guide.